COMPREHENSIVE RESEARCH
AND STUDY GUIDE

BLOOM'S
MAJOR
SHORT
STORY
WRITERS

Edgar Allan
Poe

EDITED AND WITH AN
INTRODUCTION BY HAROLD BLOOM

CURRENTLY AVAILABLE

~~~~ 
## BLOOM'S MAJOR DRAMATISTS

Anton Chekhov
Henrik Ibsen
Arthur Miller
Eugene O'Neill
Shakespeare's Comedies
Shakespeare's Histories
Shakespeare's Romances
Shakespeare's Tragedies
George Bernard Shaw
Tennessee Williams
☙

~~~~
BLOOM'S MAJOR NOVELISTS

Jane Austen
The Brontës
Willa Cather
Charles Dickens
William Faulkner
F. Scott Fitzgerald
Nathaniel Hawthorne
Ernest Hemingway
Toni Morrison
John Steinbeck
Mark Twain
Alice Walker
☙

~~~~
## BLOOM'S MAJOR SHORT STORY WRITERS

William Faulkner
F. Scott Fitzgerald
Ernest Hemingway
O. Henry
James Joyce
Herman Melville
Flannery O'Connor
Edgar Allan Poe
J. D. Salinger
John Steinbeck
Mark Twain
Eudora Welty
☙

~~~~
BLOOM'S MAJOR WORLD POETS

Geoffrey Chaucer
Emily Dickinson
John Donne
T. S. Eliot
Robert Frost
Langston Hughes
John Milton
Edgar Allan Poe
Shakespeare's Poems & Sonnets
Alfred, Lord Tennyson
Walt Whitman
William Wordsworth
☙

~~~~
BLOOM'S NOTES

The Adventures of Huckleberry Finn
Aeneid
The Age of Innocence
Animal Farm
The Autobiography of Malcolm X
The Awakening
Beloved
Beowulf
Billy Budd, Benito Cereno, & Bartleby the Scrivener
Brave New World
The Catcher in the Rye
Crime and Punishment
The Crucible

Death of a Salesman
A Farewell to Arms
Frankenstein
The Grapes of Wrath
Great Expectations
The Great Gatsby
Gulliver's Travels
Hamlet
Heart of Darkness & The Secret Sharer
Henry IV, Part One
I Know Why the Caged Bird Sings
Iliad
Inferno
Invisible Man
Jane Eyre
Julius Caesar

King Lear
Lord of the Flies
Macbeth
A Midsummer Night's Dream
Moby-Dick
Native Son
Nineteen Eighty-Four
Odyssey
Oedipus Plays
Of Mice and Men
The Old Man and the Sea
Othello
Paradise Lost
A Portrait of the Artist as a Young Man
The Portrait of a Lady

Pride and Prejudice
The Red Badge of Courage
Romeo and Juliet
The Scarlet Letter
Silas Marner
The Sound and the Fury
The Sun Also Rises
A Tale of Two Cities
Tess of the D'Urbervilles
Their Eyes Were Watching God
To Kill a Mockingbird
Uncle Tom's Cabin
Wuthering Heights
☙

COMPREHENSIVE RESEARCH
AND STUDY GUIDE

BLOOM'S
MAJOR
SHORT STORY
WRITERS

Edgar Allan
Poe

EDITED AND WITH AN INTRODUCTION BY HAROLD BLOOM

3 5 7 9 8 6 4 2

Library of Congress Cataloging-in-Publication Data

Edgar Allan Poe / edited and with an introduction by Harold Bloom.
p.   cm. — (Bloom's major short story writers)
Includes bibliographical references and index.
ISBN 0-7910-5117-X (hc.)
1. Poe, Edgar Allan, 1809-1849—Criticism and interpretation.
2. Horror tales, American—History and criticism.   3. Short story.
I. Bloom, Harold.   II. Series.
PS2638.E32   1998
818'.309—dc21
98-41380
CIP

Chelsea House Publishers
1974 Sproul Road, Suite 400
Broomall, PA 19008-0914

CONTRIBUTING EDITOR: Gwendolyn Bellerman

Contents

User's Guide

This volume is designed to present biographical, critical, and bibliographical information on the author's best-known or most important short stories. Following Harold Bloom's editor's note and introduction are a detailed biography of the author, discussing major life events and important literary accomplishments. A plot summary of each short story follows, tracing significant themes, patterns, and motifs in the work, and an annotated list of characters supplies brief information on the main characters in each story.

A selection of critical extracts, derived from previously published material from leading critics, analyzes aspects of each short story. The extracts consist of statements from the author, if available, early reviews of the work, and later evaluations up to the present. A bibliography of the author's writings (including a complete list of all books written, cowritten, edited, and translated), a list of additional books and articles on the author and the work, and an index of themes and ideas in the author's writings conclude the volume.

~

Harold Bloom is Sterling Professor of the Humanities at Yale University and Henry W. and Albert A. Berg Professor of English at the New York University Graduate School. He is the author of over 20 books and the editor of more than 30 anthologies of literary criticism.

Professor Bloom's works include *Shelley's Mythmaking* (1959), *The Visionary Company* (1961), *Blake's Apocalypse* (1963), *Yeats* (1970), *A Map of Misreading* (1975), *Kabbalah and Criticism* (1975), and *Agon: Toward a Theory of Revisionism* (1982). *The Anxiety of Influence* (1973) sets forth Professor Bloom's provocative theory of the literary relationships between the great writers and their predecessors. His most recent books include *The American Religion* (1992), *The Western Canon* (1994), *Omens of Millennium: The Gnosis of Angels, Dreams, and Resurrection* (1996), and *Shakespeare: The Invention of the Human* (1998).

Professor Bloom earned his Ph.D. from Yale University in 1955 and has served on the Yale faculty since then. He is a 1985 MacArthur Foundation Award recipient and served as the Charles Eliot Norton Professor of Poetry at Harvard University in 1987-88. He is currently the editor of other Chelsea House series in literary criticism, including BLOOM'S NOTES, BLOOM'S MAJOR POETS, MAJOR LITERARY CHARACTERS, MODERN CRITICAL VIEWS, MODERN CRITICAL INTERPRETATIONS, and WOMEN WRITERS OF ENGLISH AND THEIR WORKS.

Editor's Note

My Introduction, which will hardly please Poe's admirers, ascribes his inescapability and universality to his mythic inventiveness, particularly in the realm of nightmare.

As some twenty-seven Critical Views are included in this volume, I will comment here only upon those that I myself find particularly provocative.

Baudelaire inaugurated French Poe, who continues to reverberate in the extracts here from T.S. Eliot and Eliot's disciple, Allen Tate. The novelist D.H. Lawrence, certainly Poe's best critic, rightly sees "The Fall of the House of Usher" as an instance of self-disintegration.

The histrionic element in Poe is accurately noted by N. Bryllion Fagin, while the poet Richard Wilbur deftly interprets "The Haunted Palace," supposedly an effusion of Roderick Usher's.

Nina Baym finds Poe's true center in characters self-crazed by their own fantasies, after which Daniel Hoffman and Guy Davenport analyze Poe's symbolism.

In a brilliant reading of monologue as a form, Ken Frieden illuminates "The Tell-Tale Heart," while Christopher Benfey further explores the paradoxes of that story.

Introduction

HAROLD BLOOM

Poe is an inescapable writer, but not a good one. He is, except perhaps for Mark Twain, the most popular of all American authors. The experience of reading Poe's stories out loud to oneself is not aesthetically very satisfying. Greatly improved by translation (even into English), Poe's tales have transcended their palpable flaws in style and diction. As editor of this volume, I am acutely conscious that I am in the critical minority with regard to Poe. Having just reread four of his most famous stories— "The Fall of the House of Usher," "The Tell-Tale Heart," "The Cask of Amontillado," "The Pit and the Pendulum"—I find myself challenged to account for the gap between Poe's world-wide influence and the literary inadequacy of even his best work.

Mythopoeic power in the great Romantics—Blake and Shelley among them—is accompanied by astonishing eloquence. No one— not even a skeptic like me—can deny Poe's strength and fecundity as a mythmaker. The mythic force of Poe's tales, even of his dreadful poems, remains undiminished. Try retelling "The Fall of the House of Usher" to a friend (if you can find one who hasn't read it, or seen a film version!), and I think it likely that you may improve upon the original. The exact words of the story scarcely matter, and yet the fable persists, and continues to enchant millions around the globe. I cannot think of any other author who writes so abominably, and yet is so clearly destined to go on being canonical.

Harry Levin, forty years ago, observed that Poe's writing "smells of the thesaurus." That was a kind judgment, since Poe's synonyms rarely are appropriate for one another. Poe's partisans excuse him by arguing that he was always in a hurry because of financial pressures, but I doubt that more leisure would have improved his style. I quote, utterly at random, from "The Fall of the House of Usher," and again I urge that you read this out loud to yourself, since that forces one to slow down and listen:

> I have said that the sole effect of my somewhat childish experiment— that of looking down the tarn—had been to deepen the first singular impression. There can be no doubt that the consciousness of the

rapid increase of my superstition—for why should I not so term it?—served mainly to accelerate the increase itself. Such, I have long known, is the paradoxical law of all sentiments having terror as a basis. And it might have been for this reason only, that, when I again uplifted my eyes to the house itself, from its image in the pool, there grew in my mind a strange fancy—a fancy so ridiculous, indeed, that I but mention it to show the vivid force of the sensations which oppressed me. I had so worked upon my imagination as really to believe that about the whole mansion and domain there hung an atmosphere which had no affinity with the air of heaven, but which had reeked up from the decayed trees, and the gray wall, and the silent tarn—a pestilent and mystic vapour, dull, sluggish, faintly discernible, and leaden-hued.

That "pestilent and mystic vapour, dull, sluggish, faintly discernible, and leaden-hued" could be marketed as Essence of Poe, if we bottled it. We would do equally well had Poe written: "pestilent and mystic Roderick Usher, dull, sluggish, faintly discernible, and leaden-hued," since poor Roderick is only a vapour, but then so is the entire story. Critics agitate themselves as to whether the Lady Madeline Usher is a vampire, or whether she and Roderick have indulged a taste for incest. Everyone in Poe is more or less a vampire, but characters in Poe, particularly the Ushers, hardly seem robust enough to make love. When the undead Madeline "with a low moaning cry, fell heavily inward upon the person of her brother," that may well have been both their initial and final physical contact, more than sufficient to destroy them both. Their relationship is as vaporous as the rest of the story, including its narrator, himself very dim.

Still, however I scoff, "The Fall of the House of Usher" persists. Where does one locate its mythic appeal? Poe achieves the universality of nightmare, and that is certainly an attainment, though not necessarily a literary one. We have other authors who have given us peculiarly American nightmares, but only Poe's phantasmagorias export equally well to France and to Russia, to Singapore and to Sumatra. Nightmares are Poe's staple: he frightens children, who discover dreadful intimacies in his worst imaginings. Murderer and victim alike are equally ghastly in "The Tell-Tale Heart" and "The Cask of Amontillado." I remember, as a child, being badly upset by both stories, and frightened out of sleep by the egregiously horrible "The Pit and the Pendulum." Myths of victimage, of being buried alive, of houses falling in upon one, have been more than myths throughout history, and are peculiarly disturbing in our post-Holocaust world. Something primordial in Poe tapped into a universal anguish. Perhaps it is just as well that he wrote so badly; his myths are effective enough to render his readers vulnerable to even his weakest imaginings. I at least would not want a stronger Poe. ❀

Biography of Edgar Allan Poe

(1809–1849)

Horror, despair, and the ever-present gaping of the grave: Edgar Allan Poe's life serves as the dark template of his poems and short stories. One of the most widely read American authors today, he spent his life in poverty, moving from job to job and city to city as he struggled to subdue his anxieties and irreversible alcoholism. In many ways Poe's writing is eerily prescient of the changes that have overtaken American society, the neurosis and misery, the sense of alienation and inner turmoil that drive his characters to death and murder. Influenced profoundly by Romantics like Keats, Coleridge, De Quincey, and Washington Irving, Poe's writing has given rise to some of the most prominent trends in American literature. He wrote the first detective story ("The Murders in the Rue Morgue," 1841), and brought a hitherto unknown psychological depth to tales of horror. Well before the concept of a divided consciousness became a commonplace of newspaper and magazine accounts, Poe wrote of the double self and illustrated in graphic and terrifying detail the madness and despair that can arise from inner turmoil. In many ways, Poe's obsession with the occult and mysterious world of the supernatural made the brooding darkness of the human mind an entirely new land for future generations of writers to explore.

Edgar Allan Poe was born in Boston on January 19, 1809, the son of actors. His father David was an moody, unstable alcoholic who abandoned his wife and family when Edgar was two years old. Poe's mother, Elizabeth, died of tuberculosis within a year of David's desertion. Poe was quickly taken in, but never officially adopted, by John and Francis Allan.

In 1826 Edgar left Richmond for the University of Virginia. After less than a year, however, Poe left the University due to the enormous drinking and gambling debts he had incurred. He returned to a stormy scene at home, and in 1827 ran away to Boston, where he arranged for the publication of his first collection of verses, *Tamerlane and Other Poems*, which were printed anonymously under the name "a Bostonian." After a short stint in the army, Poe went to live in

Baltimore with his paternal grandmother, Maria Clemm, and her young daughter Virginia. During this time he published his second selection of poems, *Al Aaraaf, Tamerlane and Other Poems.*

Poe attended the United States Military at West Point briefly during 1830 and 1831 before moving back to Baltimore to be with Mrs. Clemm. During the years from 1832 to 1835 he struggled to find a place for himself in the literary world. He published a number of short stories and won a prize for story writing in the *Baltimore Sunday Visitor,* but when John Allan died after writing Edgar out of his will, Poe was virtually destitute. It was not until he became the assistant editor of the *Southern Literary Messenger,* a prestigious journal, that he was able to secure a level of ease. It was at this time that one of the more sensational occurrences of his life took place.

On May 16, 1836, the 27-year-old Poe married his cousin Virginia, who was just short of fourteen years old. It may have been more a matter of convenience than of love; ever since the deaths of his mother and foster mother, Poe had felt an overwhelming need to have supportive, loving women near him, and the marriage to Virginia ensured that he would be able to maintain his close relationship with her and her mother. At any rate, contemporary accounts report that the Poes were a happy, loving couple despite their poverty.

Soon enough their newlywed joy was shattered. Poe was asked to leave his job as editor due to his excessive drinking and irresponsibility. His writing was not selling well, and he was reduced to writing hack work like *The Conchologist's First Book* just to make ends meet. He gained and lost a position as editor for *Burton's Gentleman's Magazine,* for which he wrote "The Fall of the House of Usher," but again was fired for his erratic behavior and drunkenness.

The year 1841 was in many ways the high point of Poe's life, and may be seen as the only happy period in his adult life. He was hired as editor of *Graham's Literary Magazine* at the affluent salary of $800 per year, and during his tenure the circulation of the magazine improved tremendously. His writing also went well, and he wrote some of his most famous stories, including "The Murders in the Rue Morgue," "The Mask of the Red Death," and "A Descent into the Maelström." He and Virginia lived with her mother in a comfortable house in Philadelphia, and he seemed to have completely controlled his drinking. But like the happiness of the characters in his stories, this calm and security was not to last.

In 1842 Virginia burst a blood vessel while singing, and hovered on the verge of death. She entered a terrible spiral of recovery and illness, and Poe despaired of her life. He began drinking heavily, and left *Graham's Magazine*. It was during this time of terrible pain that Poe wrote some of his best work, including "The Pit and the Pendulum," "The Tell-Tale Heart," and "The Gold-Bug." By 1844 Virginia had recovered enough for the couple to move to New York.

Poe published "The Raven" in 1845 to enormous critical and popular acclaim. Shortly thereafter, however, his life entered an irreversible downward spiral. The Poes were desperately poor, and in 1847 Virginia died of tuberculosis. He grieved uncontrollably for his wife, and all attempts at other relationships failed. He feared for his own sanity, and at one point tried to kill himself with an overdose of laudanum. Long periods of total derangement and hallucination followed, and in 1849 he was found unconscious, drunk, and beaten, lying over a barrel in an alleyway in Baltimore. He was taken to a charity hospital, where he lingered, regained consciousness briefly and died on October 7. His last, agonized, words were "Lord, help my poor soul!"

Chivalrous towards women, courteous and charming when not in his cups, brilliant in his work, yet one of the most deeply tormented figures of American literature, Edgar Allan Poe blazed darkly through life. He became a major influence upon French Symbolists such as Rimbaud, Mallarmé, and Verlaine, who considered Poe the first modern poet. His effect upon American writers is incalculable, and is shown in the dark, psychological writings of Bierce, Melville, Faulkner, and others. While his stories may seem bizarre, even grotesque, the artistry of his work, his philosophy and esthetics have inspired thinkers such as Frederick Nietzsche, George Bernard Shaw and even the Surrealist painters. Poe's life was poignant, eccentric, and morbid, a fantasy of the grotesque. His writings, far from haunting us with the unknown, bring us face to face with our own devils, and through our own terror we come to see a powerful, frightening side of our own consciousness. ❀

Plot Summary of
"The Fall of the House of Usher"

In many ways "The Fall of the House of Usher" shows Poe at his greatest artistic powers. His manipulation of atmosphere and carefully controlled structure lend an overwhelming force to this "tale of terror," and although the plot of the story remains somewhat thin, his development of character makes this an unerring psychological allegory whose effect is devastating.

The opening five paragraphs of "The Fall of the House of Usher" establish the dark, frightening atmosphere that surrounds the ancestral mansion of the Ushers. The narrator, a childhood companion of Roderick Usher's, has arrived in answer to a dramatic letter begging him to help his friend in a time of illness and despair. The narrator refers to the "sense of insufferable gloom" that pervades the house and its surroundings, a gloom essential to the gothic tale. The term *Gothic* refers to a literary genre characterized by an overall atmosphere of dread, combining terror with horror and mystery as it emphasizes the mysterious, the supernatural, the despairing man adrift in a dark world. Captain Ahab, in Herman Melville's *Moby Dick*, exemplifies the gothic hero's descent into horror and ultimate annihilation when confronted with a spectral and overwhelming force of evil. Poe himself characterized "Usher" as a "grotesque," a setting in which the world is completely unlike the familiar, in which inanimate objects possess powers and sentience equal to those of humans and animals.

The opening scene also introduces the concept of the double, the twin, the mirror-image, that Poe found so effective. The narrator looks first at the house not directly, but as it is reflected in the dismal tarn at its feet. He notes its "vacant and eye-like windows," its facade covered with web-like fungi, and the fissure that runs from the top of the house to the bottom, all images that will recur late in the tale. Just as the twins Madeleine and Roderick Usher mirror each other in spirit and appearance, so too does the house itself serve as the image of Usher's mental decay and collapse. Later in the tale, Usher will read the poem of the "Haunted Palace," whose deterioration echoes that of both the House of Usher and Roderick Usher himself.

With these intricate mirrorings, Poe is able to complete the most important technique of composition, that of unity. The reflections that echo back and forth serve to focus the reader's attention on the central themes of the tale, as for example, the mirroring between Roderick Usher and his sister gives the reader greater insight into the collapse of both. Poe stressed that every word of a piece of fiction should contribute to a "unique single effect," and in the "The Fall of the House of Usher" every detail of the opening description and narrator's reaction leads unfailingly to the final disaster. Poe achieves his structural symmetry by locating certain elements of the plot in the opening and the closing sections of the story. Madeleine Usher appears only in the beginning and in the climactic moment, the tarn reflects the image of the house and in the end swallows the collapsing ruin, and the fissure signaling the instability of the Ushers themselves reappears at the end to destroy the House. Just as the Usher family is without "collateral issue," or side-branches, so too is the unity of the story free of any extraneous elements.

Running like a dark thread throughout the story is the overwhelming sense of terror that chokes the narrator and reader. As Roderick Usher says, "I feel that the period will sooner or later arrive when I must abandon life and reason together, in some struggle with the grim phantasm, FEAR." Poe's highly emotional language, which lends the tale a sort of oppressive, hysterical terror, envelops both the narrator and the reader in this sense of the "grim phantasm." Every detail of description, every reaction by the characters, contributes to this unity of atmosphere and tone.

After contemplating the deteriorating house in the dark lake, the narrator enters into its gothic archway and is led through "many dark and intricate passages" to the studio of the master. This movement, from the external impression of a house in decay to the inner darkness of its owner, foreshadows the movement of the tale itself. The narrator finds his friend Roderick Usher transformed by his illness into the image of a living corpse: "a cadaverousness of complexion . . . a ghastly pallor," combined with a hyper-sensitivity of the senses that makes him unable to leave his home. Usher explains that his only companion for many years has been his twin sister Madeleine, who is now suffering herself from a severe illness. However, while Roderick is overly sensitive to every passing stimulus, like a too-tight lute string vibrating in the breeze, his sister Madeleine is cataleptical, in other words unable to feel any sensation. Her brother fears her imminent collapse, and indeed on the very night of the narrator's arrival she takes to her bed, dying of an inherited malaise.

During the next few days Usher and the narrator attempt to lighten the melancholy air of the house by painting, reading and playing music. Their efforts are in vain, however, as Usher's painting acts only to illustrate his terror-stricken mind, his music to display his disordered imagination, and his poetry to serve as a reminder of the collapse of his family and home. Soon after the narrator arrives the Lady Madeleine dies, and her brother and his friend carry her coffin to a vault deep in the catacombs under the house. Before screwing down the lid, the narrator beholds Madeleine's face for the first time, and is amazed by the "mockery of a faint blush upon the bosom and face," and by the striking similarity between the woman and her brother. Usher murmurs that she and he had exchanged "sympathies of a scarcely intelligible nature," which has led many critics to infer that the relationship between the two was not only obsessive but incestuous.

After the entombment of his sister, Roderick Usher becomes ever more distracted and mentally disordered, until the night when a tremendous storm or whirlwind gathers around the house. The narrator is aroused by a sensation of irrepressible horror, as though an evil spirit were crouching upon his heart. He rises to pace about his chamber, and soon Roderick enters in a state of hysterical panic. The narrator attempts to soothe him by reading from an Arthurian romance about a hero conquering a dragon, but soon an eerie congruence begins to occur between the sounds described in the romance and those arising deep within the mansion. The clanging of the hero's shield is echoed by a brassy clamor from the vaults, the shrieking of the dragon is the counterpart to a horrible screaming or grating sound far off in the distance. The narrator's fear at these coincidences is as nothing compared to that of Roderick Usher, who stares fixedly ahead, murmuring that he has heard the sounds for many days, and that they come from the Lady Madeleine, whom they placed "*living in her tomb.*" As the terrible sounds approach, Usher's voice rises to a shout as he leaps up with staring eyes: "Madman! *I tell you that she stands now without the door!*" Just then the heavy black doors of the chamber are forced open by a gust of wind, revealing Madeleine in a bloody shroud "trembling and reeling to and fro on the threshold." With a low cry she falls forward upon her brother, and both collapse lifeless upon the floor. Consumed by horror, the narrator flees into the storm-wracked night. He turns back for a final glimpse, and sees the blood-red moon rising full behind the mansion. As he gazes, the fissure he saw on his first view of the house extending from roof to foundation widens, splitting the house in half until it thunders down into the dank tarn, which covers the House of Usher forever in its depths.

In that the house itself is often read as symbolic of Roderick Usher's own mental state, the fatal fissure is seen as arising from his disordered mind. He has attempted to bury his other half, the twin who is both alive and dead, and such a schism destroys him. Some critics have also seen Madeleine as the embodiment of the spiritual or ethereal side of Usher's nature, without which he becomes a sort of insensate zombie. Their simultaneous collapse returns the twins to the unity they possessed before birth, except that here the unity is that of Death triumphant. The forces of Life and Reason have been conquered by Death and Madness, a physical, intellectual and moral fall in which the power of fear defeats the material world. ❀

List of Characters in
"The Fall of the House of Usher"

Roderick Usher

Psychologically and physically isolated in his dark home, the scion of an old and prestigious family, Roderick Usher has not left the house in many years due to an unnamed nervous malady. He and his sister are the only remaining members of the illustrious House of Usher, a family noted both for its "peculiar sensibility of temperament" and its lack of family branches. He is unable to bear any untoward outside stimulation, and is possessed by an overwhelming sense of fear and imminent emotional and intellectual collapse. As the story progresses, Usher proceeds ever deeper into a sort of schizophrenic terror, despite his friend's efforts to distract him with music, painting, and literature. In the end, his final madness is precipitated by his guilt over his premature interment of his sister, Madeline, and his refusal to exhume her, despite his knowledge of her struggles within the coffin. It has often been noted that Roderick Usher's fine hair, broad brows, and dark, brilliant eyes resemble those of Poe himself. If so, then reading "The Fall of the House of Usher" as a tale of the introverted, artistic soul tormented and unable to function in the ordinary world may provide insight into Poe's own struggles as a writer.

Madeline Usher

The twin sister of Roderick Usher, Madeline appears only briefly at the beginning of the story, pacing slowly across the far end of a chamber. She is consumed by a wasting illness of a "cataleptical character," and shortly after the narrator arrives she dies. For fear that she might be exhumed by the sinister family doctor, Usher insists that he and the narrator must entomb her for two weeks in one of the underground vaults of the house. But he has pronounced her death prematurely, and her superhuman desire to live leads her to force her way out of the vault and stagger to the upper chambers, where she falls upon her brother in her death-throes. Throughout the tale Madeline functions as the image of "life-in-death," the living will enshrouded within the walking corpse. Madeline and Roderick function as one consciousness in two bodies, whose simultaneous death allows them to reach once again a unity of a soul divided only in life.

Narrator

Unnamed and unknown, the narrator of "The Fall of the House of Usher" is identified only as a childhood friend of Roderick Usher. His reliance on natural and rational explanations for the supernatural events at the fearful mansion throws Usher's morbidly artistic temperament into high relief, just as his ultimate infection by the surrounding miasma of terror gives the reader psychological insight into Usher's ultimate collapse. The narrator here is the symbol of rational convention, the man who attributes his depressed spirits upon seeing the House of Usher in the tarn to the influence of "very simple natural objects," and Usher's general state of collapse to hypochondria. In the end, even the "rational" narrator has been enwrapped in the atmosphere of lurid terror. His reason is unable to account for the re-appearance of the Lady Madeline and subsequent collapse of the House of Usher and he flees "aghast." ❀

Critical Views on
"The Fall of the House of Usher"

NINA BAYM ON REALITY AND MADNESS

[Nina Baym is one of the best-known Feminist scholars in America, as well as a noted scholar of American literature. She has received fellowships from the Guggenheim Foundation and the National Endowment for the Humanities, and has been an associate of the Center for Advanced Studies at Princeton University. Since 1963 she has taught at the University of Illinois at Urbana-Champaign. She is the author of *The Shape of Hawthorne's Career* and the co-editor of the *Norton Anthology of American Literature and the Columbia History of the United States*. Baym argues with previous Poe scholars who have said that Poe was concerned with the "duality of inner versus outer reality," claiming that he was actually envisioning the character driven mad by his own imaginative powers.]

I suggest that we suspend our view of Poe as concerned with the romantic problem of imposing the self on an intractable reality. We should see him, instead, concerned with another and equally "romantic" problem: investigating the nature of imagination itself. It is wonderful, comments the narrator of "Berenice," "how total an inversion took place in the character of my commonest thought. The politics of the world affected me as visions, and as visions only, while the wild ideas of the land of dreams became, in turn, not the material of my every-day existence, but in very deed that existence utterly and solely in itself." The setting of a Poe story, then, is not an external world at all, but the world of the imagination made substantial for the purpose of coming to know it better. The drama of the setting is the drama of the spectator because he has created, and imagined, that setting. And if the plot of the Poe fiction is the destruction of the spectator by the environment, we are not resorting to a paradox to say that the plot is thus a plot of self-destruction. The character is destroyed, not by outside reality, but by his own imagination.

The imagination, it will be remembered, was conceived by contemporary psychology as literally an image-making power, and thought was believed to be constructed from these images. For Locke, these pictures, though made by the imagination, derived from information about the external world transmitted by the senses. For the pure idealist, the derivation of the pictures was total mystery, and the pictures might in all logic have no relation to anything outside the imagination. For the "romantic," who occupied a middle position, the pictures that result from information provided by the senses come about without the operation of imagination. Imagination is saved for the higher task of deriving pictures from contact with a second, non-sensuous world. There are a variety of possible relationships between the data of sense and the data of imagination, and to the problems of such relationships many romantic writers attended, notably in our country the Transcendentalist. But for others the reality seen by the imagination is the more important, is the specific province of the artist, and this imagined reality constitutes the totality of Poe's concern.

The "safety exit" of the romantic theory was, of course, the conviction that the withdrawal into the imagination meant a freeing, a mingling of the self with God and all the universal currents of Being, so that the retreat into self and imagination would result in an ecstatic freedom. Our Transcendentalists saw the conclusion of the imaginative retreat as a rejuvenated return into everyday reality, a reality now transfigured by the radiant imagination. A more somber romantic imagination, like Melville's, was not so optimistic about the transfiguration but did not seem to doubt that the retreat into self and imagination rendered up a truth, however black a truth it might be.

But for Poe there is liberation into no further reality at all, neither glorious nor absurd. The journey of the soul away from reality and into its own imaginative depths ends within an imagination clearly pictured as a destroying prison. The poet becomes the captive of his fantasies, and these fantasies do not lead back out into the external world, nor are they ideally beautiful. "How is it," muses the narrator of "Berenice," "that from beauty I have derived a type of unloveliness?" The narrator of "Ligeia" confesses himself a slave to opium. Even in the fairyland gardens of "Eleanora," when the couple falls in love, a cloud of silver and crimson (curtain colors) descends over the valley, "shutting us up, as if forever, within a magic prison-house of grandeur and glory." Grandeur and glory, but a prison house too.

And in "Eleanora," as in so many Poe stories, the narrator begins by asserting, or too vehemently denying (with the same effect) his madness. Instead of liberation through the mind, incarceration in the mind; instead of beauty, imprisonment in images of horror. I suggest that in the Poe story we have a progress which begins as the romantic journey to transcendent truth, or for Poe, beauty, but which turns midway into the progress of the soul to madness. The passivity of the chief character now becomes meaningful. This is the passivity of the captive will, the will which has lost or relinquished control of the total being to the image-making power.

—Baym, Nina. "The Function of Poe's Pictorialism." *The South Atlantic Quarterly* 65 (1966): 47–54.

T. S. ELIOT ON POE'S INFLUENCES

[T. S. Eliot's literary talents were profuse, ranging from poetry to drama to criticism. His first poem, "The Love Song of J. Alfred Prufrock," written in 1915, is still enormously popular, and frequently anthologized. Other works include the poem *The Waste Land,* his play *Murder in the Cathedral,* and a volume of criticism, *The Use of Poetry and the Use of Criticism.* Eliot (1888–1965) was honored with a Nobel Prize for literature in 1948. "From Poe to Valery," Eliot's only major essay on Poe, describes Poe's influence on three generations of French poets, most particularly Baudelaire, Mallarmé, and Valéry. In this section he describes the influence that Poe has had on a variety of authors and literary genres.]

As for the prose, it is recognized that Poe's tales had great influence upon some types of popular fiction. So far as detective fiction is concerned, nearly everything can be traced to two authors: Poe and Wilkie Collins. The two influences sometimes occur, but are also responsible for two different types of detective. The efficient professional policeman originates with Collins, the brilliant and eccentric amateur with Poe. Conan Doyle owes much to Poe, and not merely to Monsieur Dupin of *The Murders in the Rue Morgue.* Sherlock

Holmes was deceiving Watson when he told him that he had bought his Stradivarius violin for a few shillings at a second-hand shop in the Tottenham Court Road. He found that violin in the ruins of the house of Usher. There is a close similarity between the musical exercises of Holmes and those of Roderick Usher: those wild and irregular improvisations which, while on one occasion they sent Watson off to sleep, must have been excruciating to any ear trained to music. It seems to me probable that the romances of improbable and incredible adventure of Rider Haggard found their inspiration in Poe—and Haggard himself had imitators enough. I think it equally likely that H. G. Wells, in his early romances of scientific exploration and invention, owed much to the stimulus of some of Poe's narratives—*Gordon Pym*, or *A Descent into the Maelström* for example, or *The Facts in the Case of Monsieur Valdemar*. The compilation of evidence I leave to those who are interested to pursue the enquiry. But I fear that nowadays too few readers open "She" or "The War of the Worlds" or "The Time Machine": fewer still are capable of being thrilled by their predecessors.

—Eliot, T. S. *From Poe to Valery*, New York: Harcourt, Brace and Company, 1948, pp. 10–11.

D. H. LAWRENCE ON RODERICK USHER'S LOSS OF SELF

[D. H. Lawrence's most influential novels include *The White Peacock, Sons and Lovers*, and *Lady Chatterley's Lover*, which was long banned in the United States and England because of its frank discussions of sexuality. Lawrence (1885–1930) also wrote *Studies in Classic American Literature*, an enormously influential critical work. His reading of Poe emphasizes Poe's insight into the disintegration of the soul of modern humans, with all of their neurosis and frustrations. This excerpt was originally published in 1919 in the journal *The English Review*, before being expanded into its present form. Lawrence saw Roderick Usher as having lost his "centrality of self," in his mystical union with his sister. Because of this loss, Usher has become morbidly sensitive to the influence of his atmosphere and its "vegetable sentience."]

It is a question how much, once the true centrality of the self is broken, the instrumental consciousness of man can register. When man becomes selfless, wafting instrumental like a harp in an open window, how much can his elemental consciousness express? The blood as it runs had its own sympathies and responses to the material world, quite apart from seeing. And the nerves we know vibrate all the while to unseen presences, unseen forces. So Roderick Usher quivers on the edge of material existence.

It is this mechanical consciousness which gives "the fervid facility of his impromptus." It is the same thing that gives Poe his extraordinary facility in versification. The absence of real central or impulsive being in himself leave him inordinately, mechanically sensitive to sounds and effects, associations of sounds, associations of rhyme, for example—mechanical, facile, having no root in any passion. It is all a secondary, meretricious process. So we get Roderick Usher's poem, *The Haunted Palace*, with its swift yet mechanical subtleties of rhyme and rhythm, its vulgarity of epithet. It is all a sort of dream-process, where the association between parts is mechanical, accidental as far as passionate meaning goes.

Usher thought that all vegetable things had sentience. Surely all material things have a *form* of sentience, even the inorganic: surely they all exist in some subtle and complicated tension of vibration which makes them sensitive to external influence and causes them to have an influence on other external objects, irrespective of contact. It is of this vibration or inorganic consciousness that Poe is master: the sleep-consciousness. Thus Roderick Usher was convinced that his whole surroundings, the stones of the house, the fungi, the water in the tarn, the very reflected image of the whole, was woven into a physical oneness with the family, condensed, as it were, into one atmosphere—the special atmosphere in which alone the Ushers could live. And it was this atmosphere which had moulded the destinies of his family.

But while ever the soul remains alive, it is the moulder and not the moulded. It is the souls of living men that subtly impregnate stones, houses, mountains, continents, and give these their subtlest form.

People only become subject to stones after having lost their integral souls.

—Lawrence, D. H. "Edgar Allan Poe." In *Studies in Classic American Literature.* New York: The Viking Press, 1923, pp. 77–78.

DARRELL ABEL ON SYMBOLISM AND ISOLATION IN THE STORY

[A professor of English at Purdue University and Franklin and Marshall College, Darrell Abel is an extremely well-known critic of early American literature. His publications include *Colonial and Early National Writing, The Moral Picturesque: Studies in Hawthorne's Fiction,* and *Masterworks of American Realism.* In "A Key to the House of Usher," Abel discusses how Poe creates the overwhelming "effect" of this story using an extensive and complex intertwining of symbols. This selection focuses on Roderick Usher as a symbol of isolation and a life force that has become so concentrated that it collapses in upon itself.]

Roderick Usher is himself a symbol of isolation, and a concentration of vitality so introverted that it utterly destroys itself. He is physically isolated. Anthropos reaches the house of Usher after a whole day's journey "through a singularly dreary tract of country" that is recognizably the same sort of domain-beyond-reality as that traversed by Childe Roland and his medieval prototypes. Arrived at the mansion, he is conducted to Usher's studio "through many dark and intricate passages." And there "the eye struggled in vain to reach the remoter angles of the chamber" in which his host received him.

Usher is psychologically isolated. Although he has invited his former "boon companion" to visit and support him in this moral crisis, clearly there has never been any conviviality in his nature. "His reserve had always been habitual and excessive," and he has now evidently become more singular, preoccupied, and aloof than before. "For many years, he had never ventured forth" from the gloomy House of Usher, wherein "he was enchained by certain superstitious impression." ("Superstitious" is the sceptical judgment of Anthropos.) Thus, although his seclusion had probably once been voluntary, it is now inescapable. His sister Madeline does not relieve his isolation; paradoxically, she intensifies it, for they are twins whose "striking similitude" and "sympathies of a scarcely intelligible nature" eliminate that margin of difference which is necessary to social relationship between persons. They are not two persons, but one consciousness in two bodies, each mirroring the other, intensifying the introversion of the family character. Further, no collateral branches of the family survive; all the life of the Ushers is flickering to extinction in these feeble representatives. Therefore no wonder that Anthropos cannot connect his host's appearance "with any idea of a simple humanity."

The isolation and concentration of the vitality of the Ushers had brought about the decay of the line. Formerly the family energies had found magnificently varied expression: "His very ancient family had been noted, time out of mind, for a peculiar sensibility of temperament; displaying itself, through long ages, in many works of exalted art, and manifested, of late, in repeated deeds of munificent yet unobtrusive charity, as well as in a passionate devotion to the intricacies, perhaps even more than to the orthodox and easily recognizable beauties, of musical science." For all the splendid flowering of this "peculiar sensibility," its devotion to intricacies was a fatal weakness; in tending inward to more hidden channels of expression, the family sensibility had become in its current representative morbidity introverted from lack of proper object and exercise, and its only flowers were flowers of evil. It was fretting Roderick Usher to death: "He suffered much from a morbid acuteness of the senses; the most insipid food was alone endurable; he could wear only garments of a certain texture; the odors of all flowers were oppressive; his eyes were tortured by even a faint light; and there were but peculiar sounds, and these from stringed instruments, which did not inspire him with horror." These specifications detail the hyper-acuity but progressive desuetude of his five senses. The sum of things which these five senses convey to a man is the sum of physical life; the relinquishment of their use in the relinquishment of life itself. The hyper-acuity of Roderick's Usher's sense was caused by the introverted concentration of the family energies; the inhibition of his senses was caused by the physical and psychological isolation of Usher. It is noteworthy that the only willing use he makes of his senses is a morbid one—not to sustain and positively experience life, but to project his "distempered ideality" on canvas and in music. This morbid use of faculties which ought to sustain and express life shows that, as Life progressively loses its hold on Roderick Usher, Death as steadily asserts its empery over him. The central action and symbolism of the tale dramatize this contest between Life and Death for the possession of Roderick Usher.

—Abel, Darrel. "A Key to the House of Usher." In *University of Toronto Quarterly* 18 (1948–49): 178–179.

ALLEN TATE ON MADELINE USHER AS A VAMPIRE

[Known as one of the leading figures in the school of literary criticism known as New Criticism, Allen Tate (1899–1979) was also a member of the Fugitives, an influential group of Southern writers including Robert Penn Warren and John Crowe Ransom. Winner of the Bollingen Prize for poetry, Tate is known equally for his verse, including "Ode to the Confederate Dead," and his criticism, such as *Reactionary Essays on Poetry and Ideas,* and *Reason in Madness.* He was also an a beloved teacher of English at the University of Minnesota. "Our Cousin, Mr. Poe" addresses many of the flaws that Tate sees in Poe's writing, but also acknowledges Poe's enormous influence, and his terrifying ability to describe the annihilation of the self. The section presented here summarizes Tate's reading of Madeleine Usher as a "vampire" whose union with her brother destroys them both.]

If we glance at "The Fall of the House of Usher" we shall be struck by a singular feature of the catastrophe. Bear in mind that Roderick and Madeline are brother and sister, and that the standard hyperaesthesia of the Poe hero acquires in Roderick a sharper reality than in any of the others, except perhaps William Wilson. His naked sensitivity to sound and light is not "regulated" to the forms of the human situation; it is a mechanism operating apart from the moral consciousness. We have here something like a capacity for mere sensation, as distinguished from sensibility, which in Usher is atrophied. In terms of the small distinction that I am offering here, sensibility keeps us in the world; sensation locks us into the self, feeding upon the disintegration of its objects and absorbing them into the void of the ego. The love, circumventing the body into the secret being of the beloved, tries to convert the spiritual object into an object of sensation: the intellect which knows and the will which possesses are unnaturally turned upon that centre of the beloved which should remain inviolate.

As the story of Usher opens, the Lady Madeline is suffering from a strange illness. She dies. Her brother has, of course, possessed her inner being, and killed her; or thinks he has, or at any rate wishes to think that she is dead. This is all a little vague: perhaps he has deliberately entombed her alive, so that she will die by suffocation—a symbolic action for extinction of being. Why has he committed this monstrous crime? Sister though she is, she is nevertheless not entirely identical with him: she has her own otherness, of however slight degree, resisting his hypertrophied will. He puts her alive, though "cataleptic," into the tomb. (Poe never uses graves, only tombs, except in "Premature Burial." His corpses, being half dead, are thus only half buried; they rise and walk again.) After some days Madeline breaks out of the tomb and confronts her brother in her bloody cerements. This is the way Poe presents the scene:

> . . . Is she not hurrying to upbraid me for my haste? Have I not heard her footsteps on the stair? Do I not distinguish the heavy and horrible beating of her heart? Madman!"—here he sprang furiously to his feet, and shrieked out his syllables, as if in his effort he were giving up his soul—"*Madman! I tell you that she now stands without the door!*"
>
> As if in the superhuman energy of his utterance there had been found the potency of a spell—the huge antique panels to which the speaker pointed threw slowly back, upon the instant, their ponderous and ebony jaws. It was the work of the rushing gust—but then without those doors there *did* stand the lofty and enshrouded figure of the Lady Madeline of Usher. There was blood upon her white robes, and the evidence of some bitter struggle upon every portion of her emaciated frame. For a moment she remained trembling to and fro upon the threshold—then, with a low moaning cry, fell heavily inward upon the person of her brother, and in her violent and now final death-agonies, bore him to the floor a corpse, and a victim to the terrors he had anticipated.

Madeline, back from the tomb, neither dead nor alive, is in the middle state of the unquiet spirit of the vampire, whose heart-beats are "heavy and horrible." There is no evidence that Poe knew any anthropology; yet in some legends of vampirism the undead has a sluggish pulse, or none at all. In falling prone upon her brother she takes the position of the vampire suffocating its victim in a sexual embrace. By these observations I do not suggest that Poe was conscious of what he was doing; had he been, he might have done it even worse. I am not saying, in other words, that Poe is offering us, in the Lady Madeline, a vampire according to Bram Stoker's specifications. An imagination of any power at all will often project its deepest assumptions about life in symbols that duplicate, without the artist's knowledge, certain meanings, the origins of which are sometimes as old as the race. If a writer ambiguously exalts the spirit over the body, and the spirit must live wholly upon another spirit, some version of the vampire legend is likely to issue as the symbolic situation.

Although the action is reported by a narrator, the fictional point of view is that of Usher: it is all seen through his eyes. But has Madeline herself not also been moving towards the cataclysmic end in the enveloping action outside the frame of the story? Has not her *will to know* done its reciprocal work upon the inner being of her brother? Their very birth had violated their unity of being. They must achieve spiritual identity in mutual destruction. The physical symbolism of the fissured house, of the miasmic air, and of the special order of nature surrounding the House of Usher and conforming to the laws of the spirits inhabiting it—all this supports the central dramatic situation, which moves towards spiritual unity through disintegration.

—Tate, Allen. "Our Cousin, Mr. Poe." In *The Forlorn Demon*. Chicago: Regnery, 1949, pp. 86–89.

LEO SPITZER ON GENDER RELATIONS IN THE STORY

[A professor of Romance philology at several Austrian and German universities, Leo Spitzer (1887–1960) also taught from 1936 to 1960 at Johns Hopkins University in Baltimore. He is the author of *Linguistics and Literary History*,

Classical and Christian Idea of World Harmony, Essays in Historical Semantics, and other critical works. "A Reinterpretation of 'The Fall of the House of Usher'" defends Poe against claims by New Critics Robert Penn Warren and Cleanth Brooks that Poe's fiction lacks tragic impact and successful characterization. Here, Spitzer examines the relationship between Roderick and Madeleine Usher, finding a reversal of gender in the two characters as Poe concentrates on the fading will to live of the Usher family.]

Roderick and Madeline, twins chained to each other by incestuous love, suffering separately but dying together, represent the male and the female principle in that decaying family whose members, by the law of sterility and destruction which rules them, must exterminate each other; Roderick has buried his sister alive, but the revived Madeline will bury Roderick under her falling body. The "fall" of the House of Usher involves not only the physical fall of the mansion, but the physical and moral fall of the two protagonists. The incestuous and sterile love of the last of the Ushers makes them turn toward each other instead of mating, as is normal for man and woman, with blood not their own. Within the mansion they never leave, they live in an absolute vacuum. In contrast to the gay comings and goings depicted in the poem recited by Roderick ("The Haunted Palace"), which reflects the former atmosphere of the mansion, we are shown only an insignificant valet of "stealthy step" and a suspect, cunning, and perplexed family physician with a "sinister countenance" (it is quite logical that Roderick, after the supposed death of his sister, should wish to keep her body as long as possible in the mansion, away from the family burial ground and exposed to the outside world, away also from the indiscreet questions of the inquisitive physician).

As to Madeline, although her physical weakness is great and she is subject to catalepsy, she does resist the curse that is weighing down the family. "Hitherto she had steadily borne up against the pressure of her malady"; and at the moment of death she shows superhuman strength: "the rending of her coffin, and the grating of the hinges of her prison, and her struggles within the coppered archway of the vault" are compared by Roderick to "the breaking of the hermit's door, and the death-cry of the dragon, and the clangor of the shield"—the feats, that is, of the doughty knight Ethelred in the romance of chivalry being read to Roderick by the narrator. Surely "the lofty and enshrouded figure of the lady Madeline of Usher," as she is presented to us in an apotheosis of majesty in death, this female Ethelred returning, blood-stained, as a "conqueror" from *her* battle with the dragon (a battle that broke the enchantment of death), is the true male and last hero of House of Usher, while her brother has in the end become a figure of passivity whose body is reduced to a trembling mass. If Roderick is the representative of death-in-life and of the death wish, Madeline becomes in the end the embodiment of life-in-death, of the will to live, indeed of a last, powerful convulsion of that will in the dying race of the Ushers.

—Spitzer, Leo. "A Reinterpretation of the 'Fall of The House of Usher'" *Comparative Literature* 4 (1952): 352–353.

RICHARD WILBUR ON "THE HAUNTED PALACE" IN THE STORY

[Richard Wilbur's first book, *The Beautiful Changes,* won a Pulitzer Prize in 1957 Since then he has published translations of Molière's *The Misanthrope* and *Tartuffe*, and has completed an edition of Poe's poems, as well as a wide variety of other works. He has taught at both Harvard and Wesleyan Universities. In "The House of Poe," originally presented as a lecture at the Library of Congress, Wilbur sees Poe's prose as "deliberate and often brilliant allegory" that developed an entirely new understanding of psychic conflict. He gives a close reading of "The Haunted Palace," the poem contained within "The Fall of the House of Usher," as symbolic of the eternal struggle taking place within the mind.]

What does it mean that Poe's heroes are invariably enclosed or circumscribed? The answer is simple: circumscription, in Poe's tales, means the exclusion from consciousness of the so-called real world, the world of time and reason and physical fact; it means the isolation of the poetic soul in visionary reverie or trance. When we find one of Poe's characters in a remote valley, or a claustral room, we know that he is in the process of dreaming his way out of the world.

Now, I want to devote the time remaining to the consideration of one kind of enclosure in Poe's tales: the mouldering mansion and its richly furnished rooms. I want to concentrate on Poe's architecture and décor to two reasons: first, because Poe's use of architecture is so frankly and provably allegorical that I should be able to be convincing about it; second, because by concentrating on one area of Poe's symbolism we shall be able to see that his stories are allegorical not only in their broad patterns, but also in their smallest details.

Let us begin with a familiar poem, "The Haunted Palace." The opening stanzas of this poem, as a number of critics have noted, make a point-by-point comparison between a building and the head of a man. The exterior of the palace represents the man's physical features; the interior represents the man's mind engaged in harmonious imaginative thought.

> In the greenest of our valleys
>   By good angels tenanted,
> Once a fair and stately palace—
>   Radiant palace—reared its head.
> In the monarch Thought's dominion—
>   It stood there!
> Never seraph spread a pinion
>   Over fabric half so fair!
>
>
> Banners yellow, glorious, golden,
>   On its roof did float and flow,
> (This—all this—was in the olden
>   Time long ago,)
> And every gentle air that dallied,
>   In that sweet day,
> Along the ramparts plumed and pallid,
>   A wingéd odor went away.
>
>
> Wanderers in that happy valley,
>   Through two luminous windows, saw
> Spirits moving musically,
>   To a lute's well-tunéd law,
> Round about a throne where, sitting,
>   Porphyrogene,
> In state his glory well befitting,
>   The ruler of the realm was seen.
>
> And all in pearl and ruby glowing
>   Was the fair palace door,

> Through which came flowing, flowing, flowing,
>   And sparkling evermore,
> A troop of Echoes, whose sweet duty
>   Was but to sing,
> In voices of surpassing beauty,
>   The wit and wisdom of their king.

I expect you observed that the two luminous windows of the palace are the eyes of a man, and that the yellow banners on the roof are his luxuriant blond hair. The "pearl and ruby" door is the man's mouth—ruby representing red lips, and pearl representing pearly white teeth. The beautiful Echoes which issue from the pearl and ruby door are the poetic utterances of the man's harmonious imagination, here symbolized as an orderly dance. The angel-guarded valley in which the palace stands, and which Poe describes as "the monarch Thought's dominion," is a symbol of the man's exclusive awareness of exalted and spiritual things. The valley is what Poe elsewhere called "that evergreen and radiant paradise which the true poet knows . . . as the limited realm of his authority, as the circumscribed Eden of his dreams."

As you all remember, the last two stanzas of the poem describe the physical and spiritual corruption of the palace and its domain, and it was to this part of the poem that Poe was referring when he told a correspondent, "By the 'Haunted Palace' I mean to imply a mind haunted by phantoms—a disordered brain." Let me read you the closing lines:

> But evil things, in robes of sorrow,
>   Assailed the monarch's high estate.
> (Ah, let us mourn!—for never morrow
>   Shall dawn upon him desolate!)
> And round about his home the glory
>   That blushed and bloomed,
> Is but a dim-remembered story
>   Of the old time entombed.
>
> And travellers, now, within that valley,
>   Through the red-litten windows see
> Vast forms, that move fantastically
>   To a discordant melody,
> While, like a ghastly rapid river,
>   Through the pale door
> A hideous throng rush out forever
>   And laugh—but smile no more.

The domain of the monarch Thought, in these final stanzas, is disrupted by civil war, and in consequence everything alters for the worse. The valley becomes barren, like the domain of Roderick Usher; the eye-like windows of the palace are no longer "luminous," but have become "red-litten"—they are like the bloodshot eyes of a madman or a drunkard. As for the mouth of our allegorized man, it is now "pale" rather than "pearl and ruby," and through it come no sweet Echoes, as before, but the wild laughter of a jangling and discordant mind.

The two states of the palace—before and after—are, as we can see, two states of mind. Poe does not make it altogether clear *why* one state of mind has given way to the other, but by recourse to similar tales and poems we can readily find the answer. The palace in its original condition expresses the imaginative harmony which the poet's soul enjoys in early childhood, when all things are viewed with a tyrannical and unchallenged subjectivity. But as the soul passes from childhood into adult life, its consciousness is more and more invaded by the corrupt and corrupting external world: it succumbs to passion, it develops a conscience, it makes concessions to reason and to objective fact. Consequently, there is civil war in the palace of the mind. The imagination must now struggle against the intellect and the moral sense; finding itself no longer able to possess the world through a serene solipsism, it strives to annihilate the outer world by turning in upon itself; it flees into irrationality and dream; and all its dreams are efforts both to recall and to simulate its primal, unfallen state. "The Haunted Palace" presents us with a possible key to the general meaning of Poe's architecture; and this key proves, if one tries it, to open every building in Poe's fiction. Roderick Usher, as you will remember, declaims "The Haunted Palace" to the visitor who tells his story, accompanying the poem with wild improvisations on the guitar. We are encouraged, therefore, to compare the palace of the poem with the house of the story; and it is no surprise to find that the Usher mansion has "vacant eye-like windows," and that there are mysterious physical sympathies between Roderick Usher and the house in which he dwells. The House of Usher *is*, in allegorical fact, the physical body of Roderick Usher, and its dim interior *is*, in fact, Roderick Usher's visionary mind.

—Wilbur, Richard, "The House of Poe." In *Poe: A Collection of Critical Essays*. Prentice-Hall Englewood Cliffs, NJ: 1967, pp. 104–107.

[A Fulbright lecturer at the University of Mainz and a professor of English at the State University of New York at
Binghamton, William Bysshe Stein is an influential scholar
of modern American Literature and eighteenth century
British literature. He is the author of *Hawthorne's Faust: The
Poetry of Melville's Late Years*. He presents here a Freudian
reading of "The Fall of the House of Usher" as a conflict
between two levels of reality, as the unconscious and conscious sides of the Usher family battle for dominance.]

Though Roderick's dissociation of personality has countless external
correlatives, from the fissure in the house to his physical and intellectual idiosyncrasies, his psychic condition, in the casual sense,
cannot be clearly understood unless it is directly related to the illness
of his twin sister. Madeline, like the other William Wilson, Ligeia,
and the pursued criminal in "The Man in the Crowd" (a story often
misread because the pursuer, the first-person narrator, is not recognized as the protagonist), is a visible embodiment of the alter ego.
She stands for the emotional or instinctive side of her brother's personality which has stagnated under the domination of the intellect
(here the tarn is a dramatic image). But as attested by the interior
poem, a synecdoche of this conflict and its outcome, these repressed
feelings will ultimately revolt against such tyranny. This turn of
events is symbolized in the disappearance of the house and its occu-
pant (the head and its monarch "Thought" in the poem) into the
storm-tossed waters of the tarn. In sum, the outraged unconscious
swallows up all conscious authority, and Roderick is rendered completely insane. As Madeline escapes her death-in-life confinement on
the literal level of action, on the psychological level the instincts (or
alter ego) attain their release. Thus the two levels of reality in the tale
are brought into perfect conjunction, and the twin motif is the
structural device that controls the final synthesis of form and,
inevitably, of tone.

—Stein, William Bysshe. "The Twin Motif in 'The Fall of the House
of Usher,'" *Modern Language Notes* 75 (1960): 110–111.

Floyd Stovall on the Role of Beauty in Poe's Prose and Poetry

[The Edgar Allan Poe Professor of English at the University of Virginia from 1955 to 1967, Floyd Stovall is one of the most prolific scholars on Poe. He has completed a critical edition of Poe's poems, *The Poems of Edgar Allan Poe*, as well as books on Walt Whitman and multiple studies, on criticism and literary history. The selection below compares Poe's poems to his prose, examining the role of beauty in each.]

In the tales I have discussed there is occasional use of what might be called the language of poetry, but the poetic principle inheres chiefly in their symmetry of form and their unity of effect. These, as Poe states in his review of *Hawthorne's Twice-Told Tales,* are characteristics which the short tale has in common with the short poem. The chief difference between the poem and the tale is in their effect. In the poem the effect is beauty, to which rhythm largely contributes; in the tale it may be a number of things—terror, horror, passion, or even truth as in the ratiocinative tale—but it cannot be the purely beautiful, which is best achieved in the metrical poem. There is one attribute which they have in common, namely, imagination, or originality, which displays itself in novelty of tone as well as of matter. These are characteristics which Poe recognizes in Hawthorne's tales, but which are perhaps best exemplified in some of his own, particularly in "Ligeia," "The Fall of the House of Usher," and "William Wilson," all of them written before the Hawthorne review. He also praises in that review what he calls Hawthorne's "essays," such as "Sights from a Steeple" and "A Rill from the Town Pump," and calls them beautiful. Unlike the tale, they have as their predominant quality repose, not effect, although they may reveal originality of thought. Poe does not mention the term "ideality" in this review, but in an earlier one he identifies it with the sentiment of poetry and defines it as that sense which also feeds his desire for knowledge. Moreover, in "The Poetic Principle" he would assert that the poetic sentiment may develop in other arts than poetry, including, as his own work demonstrates, the art of landscape gardening. His statement in the Hawthrone review that beauty can be treated better in the poem than in the prose tale must therefore not be understood as denying altogether to the prose tale the effect of beauty. Certainly Poe's own "Eleonora," to mention only one of many, has a great deal of "ideality," has beauty as one at least of its effects, and in so far as truth is also an effect, subordinates it to the level of an undercurrent.

—Stovall, Floyd. "The Poetic Principle in Prose." In *Edgar Poe the Poet*. Charlottesville: University Press of Virginia, 1969, p. 261.

Patrick F. Quinn on the Relationship between Reader, Narrator, and Roderick Usher

[An Associate Professor of English at Wellesley College, Patrick Quinn has written numerous essays on Poe. *The French Face of Edgar Poe* examines Poe's influence on French poetry and prose. In the selection reprinted here, Quinn argues that in "The Fall of the House of Usher" the terror of the soul encompasses the narrator and reader of the story as much as it does Roderick Usher himself.]

The house is underlaid with the most baffling ambiguities; not an action nor a motive has a self-evident purpose. This much at least the visitor will learn. But even as he makes his entrance he cannot clearly account for the origin of his sensations. The mist of the unknown has drifted around all he sees, and around his own mind as well. He can make things out, still recognizable, but blurred and shifting.

This is his experience from the very outset of the story. He is unable to explain the "insufferable gloom" he feels when he first comes in sight of the house. The building itself, with its vacant, eye-like windows, the rank sedge, and the dead trees—these objects should not, in themselves, oppress him. So he reasons, and in an effort to dispel this effect he studies their reversed images in the tarn that lies before the house. But this experiment only deepens his sense of gloom and foreboding. Unable to resolve the mystery here, he enters the house, in which a more complex enigma awaits him.

The two puzzles are actually very closely linked, however. Through the narrative technique he is employing in this story, Poe aligns the reader with the consciousness of the visitor to the House of Usher.

Both will participate in the experience of undefined, ambiguous, and yet very palpable evil. Usher's guest never penetrates beyond the appearances; he *lives* this experience; its significance eludes him. But the reader need not be bound by such ignorance. Poe is careful to provide details of a sort that will elucidate the mystery of the House of Usher. In other words, the opening scene of the story not only serves to establish the atmosphere of doubt and misgiving, but also to suggest the moral and psychological sources from which this atmosphere emanates. What perturbs the narrator in the appearance of the house and its grounds is that he is faced with a vision of decay. It is not the condition of death which he sees, but that of death-in-life. The house, of course, is the man, an obvious representation of Roderick Usher; and of his sister also, who in her subsequent cataleptic state is neither living nor dead.

Poe uses a strikingly paradoxical figure to describe the impression which this opening makes on the narrator. He calls his depression of soul a sensation comparable only to "the after-dream of the reveler upon opium—the hideous dropping off of the veil." But the narrator of this story does not come upon the conditions of everyday life at Usher's house. Rather the reverse: he has left everyday life behind him when he enters upon a scene in which decay and death are the presiding element. His lapse is into a dreamlike state, and a hideous veil has been let down rather than removed. However, it is only through the wrenching effect of paradox that the baffling complexities of his state of mind may be conveyed. Poe uses another device to reinforce this point. When the narrator looks into the "black and lurid tarn" and sees reflected in it the house, the sedge, and the decayed trees, he experiences a "shudder ever more thrilling than before." Why? Is it not because the unreal image, the mere reflection, seems to him more real and more threatening than the actual three-dimensional house, sedge, and trees which he has just observed before? Of the two images available, it is the shadow rather than the substance that proves to be the more terrifying. How else, except through a flat, directive statement, which would dissipate altogether the essential tone of the story, could Poe indicate that "The Fall of the House of Usher" concerns the terror of the soul, and that its visible realities are of importance only as clues to the forces concealed within that are engaged in a fatal conflict?

—Quinn, Patrick F. "'That Spectre in My Path.'" In *The French Face of Edgar Poe*. Carbondale: Southern Illinois University Press, 1957, pp. 238–240.

Plot Summary of
"The Tell-Tale Heart"

One of Poe's shortest and most concentrated tales, "The Tell-Tale Heart" is a breathless, frightening monologue of the disintegration of consciousness and conscience under the onslaught of obsession. In it we watch in horror as a man externalizes his own madness in an effort to expel and conquer his obsession, only to destroy both an innocent victim and himself. The effect of the tale is heightened by the contrast of the ravings and lunatic laughter of his narrator to the lucidly controlled and carefully constructed narrative. With this technique, Poe heightens the dramatic effect of the tale at the same time as he questions the reality of his story—its ability to faithfully mimic the outside world and the inner state of his characters.

What is perhaps most appalling about this story is its senselessness and lack of moral judgment. In it the narrator suffocates an old man, whom he professes to love, for no reason other than a diabolical obsession with the old man's so-called evil eye. The crime is revealed, but not due to the power of the police, a sense of right or wrong, or any of the forces that are believed to underlie and support society. In fact Poe carefully paints the only symbols of judgment, the police officers, as both ineffective and blind, even in the face of the narrator's obvious lunacy and violence. Only the narrator's disintegrating grasp of the outside world reveals the crime. It is this sense—that sin and insanity lurk so close to the surface of life and could exist so easily without our awareness—that lends both "The Tell-Tale Heart" and "The Cask of Amontillado" their terror. The reader cannot locate madness and violence, and may fall prey to them at any time.

The story opens with the oft-quoted lines "'True!—Nervous—very, very dreadfully nervous I had been and am; but why *will* you say that I am mad?'" His protestation is from the first one of sanity, not of innocence. He cares not whether the reader knows how horribly he stalked his victim, since in the narrator's eyes this is merely proof of his rationality, methodical planning, and precision. As in almost all of Poe's tales, the sense of irony is acute: the more the narrator asserts his rationality, the more we are convinced of his insanity. He himself admits that there is no reason for killing the old man: "Object there was none. Passion there was none. I loved the old man. He had never wronged me. He had never given me insult. For his gold I had no desire. I think it was his eye! yes, it was this!" Just as the narrator has deceived himself as to his sanity, he has deceived himself as to the purpose of the crime. For while he believes that it is the old man's filmed eye, with its gruesome blue cataract, that urges him to crime, it is actually a flaw within the narrator himself.

For seven nights the narrator creeps into the bedroom of the old man, releasing a thin ray of light upon the sleeper's face. He cannot attack, though, for "it was not the old man who vexed me, but his Evil Eye." On the eighth night, the narrator's hand slips on the latch of the lantern, and the old man starts awake at the sound, sitting bolt upright in his bed staring wildly ahead into the darkened chamber. The narrator waits for a full hour, aware of the old man's terror, before he releases a single beam of light that flares upon the horrible eye.

Many critics have commented on the association between the Evil Eye and the evil "I" of the narrator. In other words, the murderer identifies psychologically with his victim, and the focus of his rage is not actually the eye, but rather something within himself that he has projected upon the old man. Lacking any sense whatsoever of inner vision, the murderer learns about himself only by looking at the old man, and when he does so the sight is unbearable. Poe goes to great pains to make this extension of the self clear. Just before the murder, as the old man sits rigidly in his bed, heart pounding, the narrator lies in wait: "I did not hear him lie down. He was still sitting up in the bed listening;—just as I have done, night after night, hearkening to the death watches in the wall." The old man groans in his terror, just as the narrator has done so many times in the past: "I knew the sound well. Many a night . . . it has welled up from my own bosom, deepening, with its dreadful echo, the terrors that distracted me." At the moment of the crime, the murderer's yell is amplified by the old man's terrified shriek. Most important, though, is the beating of the tell-tale heart itself. Throughout the story, the pounding of an over-stressed heart drives the action forward. It is the drumming heart-beat that causes the narrator to leap forward and smother the old man, and the insistent pounding that causes him to reveal his crime to the police. Yet it is not clear whose heart he actually hears. The narrator believes it is the old man's, but clearly the heart that beats at the end can only be his own. In effect, the congruence between the two central characters leads the reader to see the old man as essentially a mirror for the narrator, an identification that emphasizes both the extent of his madness and self-denial and the solipsism of his destruction. The similarity also creates the mirroring and unity of effect he believed so important in short prose.

After the murder of the old man, the narrator dismembers his victim and hides the pieces under the floorboards of the chamber. It is here that the façade of sanity begins to crack. "There was nothing to wash out—no stain of any kind—no blood-spot whatever. . . . A tub had caught it all—ha! ha!" Madness has erupted just at the moment when the narrator believes he has freed himself from his own stain, his inner horror. The break in the narrative focuses the reader's attention on the narrator's loss of rationality, and accentuates how abnormal the contrast is between the uncontrollable wildness of the crime and the tidy clean-up that follows.

At this moment, the doorbell rings. The police have arrived in response to a neighbor's complaint of suspicious shrieks arising from the house. The narrator, talking gaily, shows the officers over the house and then sits down with them in the murdered man's bedchamber to have a chat. Soon, however, he begins to hear a ringing in his ears, a sound that resolves itself into *such a sound as a watch makes when enveloped in cotton.* It was in exactly the same words that the narrator described the old man's heart just prior to the murder. This time, however, the sound is the prelude not to the death of the victim, but the narrator's own destruction. In addition to reminding the reader of the death watches that terrified the narrator earlier in the story, this sentence emphasizes the role of time in "The Tell-Tale Heart." Poe repeatedly focuses on hours, minutes, strangely elongated moments, throughout the story. At *midnight* the killer stalks his victim, the vigil lasts for an *hour,* at *four o'clock,* when all is as dark as *midnight,* the police arrive. This repetition gives the story structural power, as well as suggesting the remorseless progression of life towards death. The cardiac rhythm is the rhythm of Death approaching.

It is when this rhythm becomes unbearable, a pounding the seems to shake the room, that the murderer explodes into a frenzy. Yet the police officers notice nothing, even when the narrator storms around the room raving and foaming. It is this lack of notice that leads the narrator to his final confession. "Was it possible they heard not? Almighty God!—no, no! They heard!—they suspected!—they knew!—they were making a mockery of my horror!. . . . I admit the deed!—tear up the planks!—here, here—it is the beating of his hideous heart." The split between his subjective reality and that of those around him has become unbridgeable, but still he cannot accept that he is mad. It is the psychological pressure of the narrator's overwhelming desire to prove his sanity, coupled with the obvious disjunction between his perception and that of others, that creates the final fissure in his psyche. His attempt to distance himself from his imbalance has succeeded only in focusing his attention upon it, a focus that destroys him. ❀

List of Characters in
"The Tell-Tale Heart"

The Narrator

Like Roderick Usher, the narrator of "The Tell-Tale Heart" has fallen ill with a mysterious ailment that has sharpened his senses to hyper-acuity: he "heard all things in the heaven and in the earth . . . many things in hell." Yet he insists that he is not mad, merely hysterically anxious and "dreadfully nervous." It is this very obsession with his own sanity that in the end illustrates to the reader the depths of the narrator's psychosis. Neither the reader nor the narrator can offer any logical explanation for the killing of the old man; in fact, the narrator professes to have loved him. The duplicity of the narrator, who can smile so charmingly as he inquires how the old man has slept every night of the dreadful death watch, is like that of Montresor in "The Cask of Amontillado," yet the narrator here is barely able to control his lunacy long enough to hide the old man's body. While Montresor is the image of the conscienceless, obsessively controlled psychopath, the narrator of "The Tell-Tale Heart" is pursued by the violence and agony of his madness as he tries and ultimately fails to project it outwards away from himself. As the destruction of the old man reflects back upon the narrator, we watch in horror the splintering of the mind.

The Old Man

All unknowing of the turmoil in his fellow-lodger's heart, the old man in this story exists as hardly more than a collection of body parts. We know only that he has done nothing to offend the narrator, that he has money, that he is fearful of robbers, and that one of his eyes is filmed over by a cataract. Confined in his dark bedroom, he is subjected to the mortal terror of the soul that arises from a nightmare, but in his case the living nightmare kills him.

The Police

Three police officers arrive at the narrator's house at 4:00 A.M. in answer to a call by a neighbor suspecting foul play. What is most shocking about the policemen is their obtuseness, their inability to see either the guilt or the madness of the narrator. As they sit talking with him and his anxiety builds, he becomes louder and more frantic in his behavior, yet they continue to smile and chat pleasantly. As in "The Cask of Amontillado," the reader is confronted with a vision of social order and justice as completely ineffectual in the face of insanity. It seems that had the narrator not been overwhelmed by his own sense of guilt, the police would have been utterly blind to the crime, as blind as the narrator is to his madness. ❀

Critical Views on
"The Tell-Tale Heart"

E. ARTHUR ROBINSON ON PSYCHOLOGY OF TIME IN POE'S STORIES

[E. Arthur Robinson's studies of Meredith, Hawthorne, Poe, and Thoreau have placed him in the forefront of scholarship on nineteenth-century American literature. He is a professor of English at the University of Rhode Island, and has also taught at the University of Idaho. In this essay Robinson analyzes Poe's tales in terms of the psychological identification between characters, as well as Poe's psychological handling of time, which entraps his characters in a emotional and physical paralysis.]

But if the old man is nearing death so too must be the narrator, who has felt the same "mortal terror" in his own bosom. This similarity serves to unify the story. In Poe's tales, extreme sensitivity of the senses usually signalizes approaching death, as in the case of Monos and of Roderick Usher. This "over acuteness" in "The Tell-Tale Heart," however, pertains chiefly to the murderer, while death comes to the man with the "vulture eye." By making the narrator dramatize his feelings in the old man, Poe draws these two motifs together. We must remember, writes one commentator upon the story, "that the criminal sought his own death in that of his victim, and that he had in effect become the man who now lies dead." Symbolically this is true. The resurgence of the beating heart shows that the horrors within himself, which the criminal attempted to identify with the old man and thus destroy, still live. In the death of the old man he sought to kill a part of himself, but his "demons" could not be exorcised through murder, for he himself is their destined victim.

From this point of view, the theme of the "Tell-Tale Heart" is self-destruction through extreme subjectivity marked paradoxically by both an excess of sensitivity and temporal solipsism. How seriously Poe could take this relativity of time and experience is evident in the poetic philosophy of his *Eureka* (1849). There time is extended almost infinitely into the life-cycle of the universe, but that cycle itself is only one heartbeat of God, who is the ultimate subjectivity. Romantically, indeed, Poe goes even further in the conclusion to *Eureka* and sees individual man becoming God, enclosing reality within himself, and acting as his own creative agent. In this state, distinction between subjective and objective fades: "The sense of individual identify will be gradually merged in the general consciousness." Destruction then becomes self-destruction, the madman and his victim being aspects of the same universal identity. Death not only is self-willed but takes on some of the sanctity of creative and hence destructive Deity. The heartbeat of the red slayer and the slain merge in Poe's metaphysical speculations as well as in the denouement of a horror story.

This extreme subjectivity, moreover, leaves the ethical problem of "The Tell-Tale Heart" unresolved. In the opening paragraph of the story is foreshadowed an issue of good and evil connected with the speaker's madness: "I heard all things in the heaven and in the earth. I heard many things in hell. How, then, am I mad?" To be dramatically functional such an issue must be related to the murder. The only outward motivation for the murder is irritation at the "vulture eye." It is the evil of the eye, not the old man (whom he "loved"), that the murderer can no longer live with, and to make sure that it is destroyed he will not kill the man while he is sleeping. What the "Evil Eye" represents that it so arouses the madman we do not know, but since he sees himself in his companion the result is self-knowledge. Vision becomes insight, the "Evil Eye" an evil "I," and the murdered man a victim sacrificed to a self-constituted deity. In this story, we have undeveloped hints of the self-abhorrence uncovered in "William Wilson" and "The Imp of the Perverse."

—Robinson, E. Arthur. "Poe's "The Tell-Tale Heart." In *Nineteenth-Century Fiction.* University of California Press, 1965, pp. 376–377.

DANIEL HOFFMAN ON TIME AND THE OEDIPAL STRUGGLE IN THE STORY

[Poet, critic and teacher, Daniel Hoffman has been a professor and poet in residence at the University of Pennsylvania since 1978. He has also taught at Temple, Columbia, and Rutgers Universities. His publications range from volumes of poetry (*An Armada of Thirty Whales, Striking the Stones*) to criticism (*Form and Fable in American Fiction, Barbarous Knowledge: Myth in the Poetry of Yeats, Graves and Muir*). He is the general editor and a contributor to the *Harvard Guide to Contemporary American Writing.* In this selection he reads the Evil Eye of the old man in "The Tell-Tale Heart" as both a Freudian father-figure and as the symbol of all-devouring Time.]

The Evil Eye is a belief as old and as dire as any in man's superstitious memory, and it usually signifies the attribution to another of a power wished for by the self. In this particular case there are other vibrations emanating from the vulture-like eye of the benign old man. Insofar as we have warrant—which I think we do—to take him as a father-figure, his Eye becomes the all-seeing surveillance of the child by the father, even by The Father. This surveillance is of course the origin of the child's conscience, the inculcation into his soul of the paternal principles of right and wrong. As such, the old man's eye becomes a ray to be feared. For if the boy deviate ever so little from the strict paths of rectitude, *it will find him out.*

Poe, in other tales, seems to be obsessed with the eye to the point of fetishism. In "Legeia" it is the lady's eyes which represent, to her husband, the total knowledge embodied in her person. By synecdoche the eyes become that which he worships. But the old man's eye is endowed with no such spiritual powers. Come to think of it, it is always referred to in the singular, as though he had but one. An old man with one all-seeing eye, an Evil Eye—from the plausible to the superstitious we pass in the text; perhaps further still to the mythical. One-eyed Odin, one-eyed because he sold his other for *knowledge.* Yet the knowledge in a father's (or a father-figure's) eye which a child most likely fears is the suspicion that he has been seen in a forbidden act, especially masturbation, or some other exercise of the libido. That above all seems to the young child to be forbidden, and therefore what an all-seeing Eye would see. Yet this old man's ocular power is never so specified. What is specified, though, is the resemblance of his one eye to that of a vulture.

Vulture, vulture. Everywhere else in Poe's work, in Poe's mind, vulture is associated with TIME, and time is associated with our mortality, our confinement in a body. The vulture-like eye of an aged man is thus an unsupportable reminder of the narrator's insufferable mortality. Could he but rid himself of its all-seeing scrutiny, he would then be free of his subjection to time.

All the more so if the father-figure in this tale be, in one of his aspects, a Father-Figure. As, to an infant, his own natural father doubtless is. So, the evil in that Evil Eye is likely a mingling of the stern reproaches of conscience with the reminder of his own subjection to time, age, and death.

—Hoffman, Daniel. "Madness!: The Tell-Tale Heart." In *Poe Poe Poe Poe Poe Poe Poe.* Garden City, NY: Doubleday & Company, Inc., 1972, pp. 228–229.

CHRISTOPHER BENFEY ON SECRECY AND KNOWLEDGE IN THE STORY

[Christopher Benfey, a professor of English at Mt. Holyoke College, is the author of *Emily Dickinson and the Problem of Others, Emily Dickinson: Lives of a Poet,* and *The Double Life of Stephen Crane.* In his essay on "The Tell-Tale Heart" Benfey discusses how secrecy and knowledge work together to ensure the old man's death and the narrator's madness.]

This is a crucial moment in the story. It shows how much the speaker's motivation has to do with secrecy, with keeping his thoughts hidden. (There is a remarkably similar moment of mute triumph in the "The Black Cat": "The glee at my heart was too strong to be restrained. I burned to say if but one word, by way of triumph.") He enters the old man's room night after night as a sort of ritual to establish this secrecy, this fact of human separateness.

And yet, for all his secrecy, our speaker claims to have access to the mind of the old man. His very privacy, his enclosedness, seem to allow him to see into the minds of other people.

> Presently I heard a slight groan, and I knew it was the groan of mortal terror. It was not a groan of pain or of grief—oh, no!—it was the low stifled sound that arises from the bottom of the soul when overcharged with awe.

We may wonder how the speaker claims to know this. The answer, he tells us, is by analogy with his own experience and its expression:

> I knew the sound well. Many a night, just at midnight, when all the world slept, it has welled up from my own bosom, deepening with its dreadful echo, the terrors that distracted me. I say I knew it well. I knew what the old man felt, and pitied him, although I chuckled at heart. I knew that he had been lying awake ever since the first slight noise.

This scene of mind reading continues a bit longer, as the killer claims to know the very words the victim is thinking:

> His fears had been ever since growing upon him. He had been trying to fancy them causeless, but could not. He had been saying to himself— "It is nothing but the wind in the chimney—it is only a mouse crossing the floor," or "it is merely a cricket which has made a single chirp." Yes, he has been trying to comfort himself with these suppositions: but he had found all in vain.

It is only after this sustained scene of mind reading versus secrecy that the old man's eye opens, and the murder is accomplished. It is precisely the breach of secrecy, the penetrating-yet-veiled eye, that seems to motivate the murder.

Poe puts unmistakable emphasis on this claim to *knowledge*: "I say I *knew* it well. I *knew* what the old man felt . . . I *knew* that he had been lying awake". It is precisely this claim to knowledge of another's mind, especially knowledge of another's feelings of pain, that has given rise to some of the most challenging philosophical reflections in our century. Wittgenstein, in a couple of classic passages in his *Philosophical Investigations*, defines the issues succinctly:

> In what sense are my sensations *private?*—Well, only I can know whether I am really in pain: another person can only surmise it. In one way this is wrong, and in another nonsense. If we are using the word "to know" as it is normally used (and how else are we to use it?), then other people very often know when I am in pain.—Yes, but all the same not with the certainty with which I know it myself!—It can't be said of me at all (except perhaps as a joke) that I *know* I am in pain. What is it supposed to mean—except perhaps that I *am* in pain?

Wittgenstein, in his characteristically dialogical style, is challenging the skeptic's claim that we cannot "know" another's pain. Wittgenstein appeals to our ordinary use of language—"and how else are we to use it?"—as opposed to some special philosophical use, and argues that it's ridiculous to claim that we never can know that another is in pain. We know this—under ordinary circumstances (the stubbed toe, the woman in labor, the burst blister)—all the time. Wittgenstein, here and elsewhere, want to cure us of our tendency to step outside our ordinary ways of living our lives, and our tendency to demand, for example, kinds of certainty that are inappropriate to our dealings with other people. (Poe seems to have something similar in mind when he insists that the events in "The Black Cat" are "ordinary.")

Poe's killers claim to have their very certainty challenged by Wittgenstein. They are always insisting on their special knowledge of others' minds, as though we had been challenging their knowledge: "I say I knew it well. I knew what the old man felt." The killer's claim, in "The Tell-Tale Heart," that he knows the man's feelings by analogy with his own—"I know that he feels x when he cries y because when I cry y I feel x"—is another of Wittgenstein's subjects:

> If one has to imagine someone else's pain on the model of one's own, this is none too easy a thing to do: for I have to imagine pain which I *do not feel* on the model of the pain which I *do feel*. That is, what I have to do is not simply to make a transition in imagination from one place of pain to another. As, from pain in the hand to pain in the arm. For I am not to imagine that I feel pain in some region of his body. (Which would also be possible.)
> Pain-behaviour can point to a painful place—but the subject of pain is the person who gives it expression.

Poe's killer makes oddly parallel claims: "I knew the sound well. Many a night, just at midnight, when all the world slept, it has welled up from my own bosom. . . . I say I knew it well. I knew what the old man felt." It does seem as though he is "imagining someone else's pain on the model of [his] own."

The skeptical view of ultimate human separateness ("We can never know for certain what another person is thinking or feeling") is intolerable to Poe's killers; their response is simply to deny it, even to the point of killing in order to prove their certainty.

—Benfey, Christopher, "Poe and the Unreadable: 'The Tell-Tale Heart.'" In *New Essays on Poe's Major Tales*. New York: Cambridge University Press, 1993, pp. 32–35.

[Ken Frieden's wide-ranging literary interests are reflected in his books, among which are *Genius and Monologue* to *Freud's Dream of Interpretation* and *Classic Yiddish Fiction*. He teaches in the department of Modern Languages and Classics at Emory University. In this selection, Frieden discusses how the contrast between the sane narrative and mad narrator of "The Tell-Tale Heart" complicates any readings of the tale as "realistic," or imitative of daily life.]

The deviant narrators of "The Tell-Tale Heart," "The Black Cat," and "The Imp of the Perverse" in some ways extend into short fiction the epistolary and conversational modes developed by Richardson, Coleridge, and their followers. Yet Poe's narrators often confront the representational illusion at the same time that they dispute the superficial claim that they are insane. In Poe's texts, the scene of madness combines with a controlled scene of writing; at exactly this point, Poe destabilizes the genre he assumes: rhetorical forms both constitute and question a conversational pretense.

On one level, Poe's mad monologues may be read as expressions of psychological realism. "The Tell-Tale Heart," for example, presents itself as the spontaneous narrative of a murderer: "True!—nervous—very, very dreadfully nervous I had been and am! But why *will* you say that I am mad? The disease had sharpened my senses—not destroyed—not dulled them. Above all was the sense of hearing acute. I heard all things in the heaven and in the earth. I heard many things in hell. How, then, mad? Hearken! And observe how healthily—how calmly I can tell you the whole story." As the scene of discourse, we may imagine ourselves in conversation with a confined lunatic. His denial of madness only intensifies the effect of his bizarre claim to have "heard all things in the heaven and in the earth." The opening words imply that we have provoked the speaker by asserting what he denies: far from being insane, he says, "the disease had sharpened my senses," and if we choose to listen, we will share his exalted mood for a few minutes. As soon as we begin to read, then, we find ourselves written into a drama in which we have accused the speaker of being nervous or mad. The narrative opens with a paradox, however, which unsettles the representational illusion. The speaker combines mad assertions with narrative lucidity and presents a disconcerting contradiction between his representing and represented pesonae. The discrepancy between sane narrator and madman perhaps shows the error of assuming that linguistic normalcy implies psychological normalcy. The narrator is mad, or at least abnormal, according to his own account, because he kills an old man for no reason. He is doubly mad when he imagines he hears the pounding of the dead man's heart and gives away the crime he had concealed. Yet the narrator tells a coherent tale, as if to demonstrate out of spite that he is sane, refuting the ordinary belief that he must be mad. This contradiction overturns mimetic conventions: a literal reading of the mad narrator shows itself to be naive because only Poe's textual pretense creates the illusion of disparity between madman and sane narrator.

—Frieden, Ken. "Poe's Narrative Monologues." In *Genius and Monologue*. Ithaca and London: Cornell University Press, 1985, pp. 160–161.

Plot Summary of
"The Cask of Amontillado"

Many critics have read "The Cask of Amontillado" as Poe's greatest short story. The story is shaped perfectly by an overwhelming sense of ambiguity in the setting, the dialogue, and even the ironic sense of opposition between the characters. Poe has crafted a tale at once about the "perfect crime" whose criminal goes unpunished and about a crime that haunts a murderer. It is this sense of unity, like that of "The Fall of the House of Usher," that lends "The Cask of Amontillado" much of its narrative force. No word is wasted as the tale builds towards its horrific and inevitable climax, no opportunity lost for double-meaning and irony, and the sense of diabolical, ruthless cruelty leaves the reader shaken.

"The Cask of Amontillado" is a soliloquy, a speech directed by the murderer Montresor to an unknown listener. Poe suggests that Montresor may be telling his tale to his confessor, "you who know so well the nature of my soul," perhaps on his deathbed, and certainly fifty years after the death of Fortunato and late in Montresor's life. If this is indeed a deathbed confession, then Montresor's utter lack of contrition, his blindness to any moral standards, rings even more horribly clear in the reader's mind. Montresor is concerned only with the skill with which he hid his determination to take revenge, his ability to smile in the face of a man he meant to kill most horribly, and such a moral vacuum challenges our understanding of what the limits are of human nature.

The tale opens during "the supreme madness of the carnival season," a time of licentiousness and freedom, when moral standards are relaxed and outrageous behavior is the norm. This setting intensifies the sense of surrealism and deception by its reference to a time of masked freedom. Just as revelers are free of moral judgment for their behavior at a Mardi Gras party, Montresor will be successful in completing a ruthless murder without external punishment.

Montresor meets Fortunato in the street, exclaiming, "My dear Fortunato, you are luckily met." Already Poe has introduced a sense of irony and amoral cruelty, as the reader knows that Montresor has vowed revenge upon his enemy and his pleasure springs only from the possibility of revenge. The meeting is indeed lucky, but not for Fortunato.

Montresor entices Fortunato to his home by claiming to have procured a cask of expensive Amontillado sherry, upon which he seeks the opinion of a wine expert. He pretends enormous concern for his enemy, worrying that the damp cold of the wind cellars will be too much for Fortunato's health. However, Fortunato's vanity has been awakened, and he refuses to allow Montresor to seek the opinion of any other connoisseur. In an ironic reversal, it is Fortunato who "possesses" himself of Montresor's arm, the victim who hurries his murderer to the scene of the murder.

Upon entering the catacombs within which the wine cellars are located, Fortunato begins to cough at the dank chill. Montresor falsely urges him back outside, worrying that the cold air will harm Fortunato's health. Montresor emphasizes how successful his enemy is and how he himself has fallen in social position: "You are rich, respected, admired, beloved; you are happy, as once I was. You are a man to be missed. For me it is no matter." Fortunato refuses, saying "the cough is a mere nothing; it will not kill me. I shall not die of a cough." True enough, and Montresor hurries him ever deeper into the tunnels, stopping only to drink a toast to Fortunato's "long life," a life whose length will only increase his suffering. It is at this time that Fortunato says that he has forgotten the Montresor coat of arms, another of his thoughtless and inconsequential insults. The arms consist of a golden human foot crushing a snake, whose fangs are buried in the heel. These arms illustrate the powerful doubling effect that echoes throughout the story. For while the foot may be seen as Montresor's ability to crush one who has insulted him, and indeed he does read it this way, the foot may also illustrate Fortunato's blithe ignorance. All unknowing he has stepped on and insulted a deadly foe, for it is impossible that he would follow Montresor into the catacombs if he knew that he had caused such dire offense. The twisting, hidden vengeance of the snake fits closely with Montresor's concealed fury and eventual revenge, as does the motto: "*Nemo me impune lacessit*" (no one offends me unpunished). Ironically, however, the arms portray a moment of mutual ruin. The snake has presumably poisoned the foot, but only at the moment in which it is itself crushed.

As they proceed further into the murky caverns, the drunken Fortunato reveals that he is a Mason, a secret society identified by a series of cryptic gestures. He refuses to believe that Montresor might also be a Mason, until his enemy reveals a trowel hidden under his cloak. The trowel, both the symbol of the Masons and of the cruel revenge Montresor is about to perpetrate, frightens Fortunato with a creeping doubt that all is not as it seems.

Soon the two reach a small cul-de-sac, ringed with the bones of the Montresor ancestors and containing only a chain and padlock bolted to the wall. In a moment, Montresor pins Fortunato to the wall and shackles him securely in place. Uncovering a pile of stones and mortar, he proceeds to coolly and calmly wall Fortunato into the chamber. Fortunato, after giving vent to a dreadful moan and then maintaining an "obstinate" silence, begins to shriek and yell. It is at this moment that Montresor reveals his only moment of doubt, of human indecision. He hesitates, trembles, and gropes inside the recess with his rapier. In this moment of psychological pressure, Montresor's subconscious rebels at what the conscious mind is doing. The horror of the dark, of the unrestrained violence of a mind set loose from social boundaries, springs upon him, and he recoils. However, by touching the "solid fabric of the catacombs" he is reassured; the material world has triumphed over the dark of the mind.

As Montresor slides the last stone into place, Fortunato calls out "*For the love of God, Montresor!*" only to be echoed by his killer, "'Yes, for the love of God!'" Montresor mocks not only Fortunato, but the concept of divine revenge, of punishment or retribution. His sense of self and domination over his world is so complete that he is unshakable. Even when his heart grows sick at his own deed he insists that it is only the dampness of vaults affecting him. Nothing can affect his mind, and his heart and soul have been as utterly conquered as the golden and intoxicated Fortunato.

"The Cask of Amontillado" is a story of the terrible dangers of knowledge and consciousness. It is Fortunato's ignorance that dooms him, his sense that he knows everything about wine and about his relationship to Montresor. And it is Montresor's obsessive need to know, to control, to direct his knowledge that empties his revenge of meaning. As he says, for a wrong to be truly redressed, the avenger must "punish with impunity. . . . It is equally unredressed when the avenger fails to make himself felt as such to him who has done the wrong." Yet Fortunato does *not* see Montresor as an avenger, only as an incomprehensible murderer. Because Fortunato never knows what terrible insult he has committed, he never knows what Montresor is avenging. Nor does Montresor "punish with impunity," for fifty years later the crime still weighs heavily on him. Although he has not been discovered or punished for his crime, Montresor has failed to achieve the perfect vengeance that compels him. At the end of his life he is obsessed with proving that he has conquered Fortunato, he himself does not "rest in peace." Yet this hint of failure on Montresor's part remains only a suggestion, with the more powerful tale being one of the impotence of justice. What makes "The Cask of Amontillado" so horrific is Montresor's absence of contrition, his ability to drive his conscience into oblivion in pursuit of a "reality" that is an illusion. We are left with the image of a brilliant intellect gone awry, an impenitent mad genius who flouts the "laws" of humanity, denies any mercy or compassion, and glories in his evil until the end of his days. ❀

List of Characters in
"The Cask of Amontillado"

Montresor

Like the protagonist in many of Poe's other short stories ("William Wilson," "The Tell-Tale Heart"), Montresor acts as the insanely "rational" man whose coolheaded intelligence masks his inability to comprehend the moral implications of his own actions. He comes from a formerly wealthy and extensive family that appears to have fallen in fortune and numbers. Obsessed with revenging himself upon Fortunato for an unknown slight, Montresor employs a facade of kindness and friendliness to mask his evil plot. He is convinced of his own cleverness, and possesses a cynically accurate grasp of human nature. His "treasure" (Montresor = *mon trésor*) is both the imaginary cask of Amontillado and his own mad genius. In the end, however, his lack of conscience dooms him to a life-long preoccupation with his crimes.

Fortunato

"Rich, respected, admired, beloved," Fortunato is a man both well-regarded and feared. However, his name, which means "the fortunate one," is ironic, since it will be his terrible misfortune to be buried alive by a diabolical madman. At some time in the past Fortunato has both injured and insulted Montresor, but we do not know the nature of these insults and injuries. When he meets Montresor at the beginning of the story, Fortunato is dressed in the brightly colored costume of a fool, with bells on his cap and stripes on his pants. Extroverted and innocent of any guile, he may be seen as the riotous alter ego to Montresor's overly controlled madness. Like Montresor, however, Fortunato is entrapped by his pride. Montresor has enticed Fortunato into the vaults by challenging his ability to judge the worth of a cask of wine, and Fortunato refuses to allow that the judgment of another man would be as accurate as his own. While Montresor's arrogance leads him away from his humanity, Fortunato's drags him downward to an inhumane death. ❀

Critical Views on
"The Cask of Amontillado"

VINCENT BURANELLI ON POE'S CHARACTERS

[Vincent Buranelli's early career included stints as a reporter for the United Press and as a newscaster and editorial writer in New York City. He is now a free-lance writer and editor. His writings include *The King and the Quaker: A Study of William Penn and James II,* and *Louis XIV.* In his work on Poe, he congratulates Poe for his "gruesome and frightening themes," which, in conjunction with Poe's skillful handling of his material, allowed Poe to turn the Gothic tale into a lasting genre. He points out, in the section below, that part of Poe's genius lies in his refusal to apply moral standards to his characters and his ability to vary his characters.]

His scope is narrow, but he has remarkable success in avoiding monotony by subtly varying the treatment of stories with much the same plot. He cannot paint his characters fully, but, according to his stated principle, he does not have to since the unveiling of character is the task of the novel. On the other hand, while his women are all alike (all being roughly a compound of his mother and his wife), his men reveal marked differences even in introductions so brief. William Wilson could not be mistaken for the narrator of "The Black Cat," or Metzengenstein for Montresor of "The Cask of Amontillado."

Poe does not touch morality. Although his aesthetic theory admits that goodness may be a by-product of art, he himself does not look for it. Sin and crime are absent from his part of his universe; and the terrible deeds that abound there are matters of psychology, abnormal psychology, not of ethics. Natural laws apply, working through human nature; the moral law does not apply. Remorse is always a compulsion, never an accusation of the moral sense after a responsible act. William Wilson destroys himself as a personality by killing his conscience, but this merely exemplifies the psychological truth that a man can be injured by the loss of this particular faculty. On the other hand, he may be able to live quite well without a conscience: Montresor does. Even "The Pit and the Pendulum" is a study of terror rather than the moral tale Poe might have made of it.

Berating Poe for putting morality out of bounds is to miss the point, for it is asking him to be a different writer than he was. It is expecting him to be approximate to Hawthorne, when his greatness is precisely to be what Hawthorne was not. It is wishing that we did not have the superb stories that Poe alone was capable of adding to the literature of the world. And these stories are not immoral; they are simply naturalistic in the best sense, not in the perverted sense of Zola, for instance, who is to a certain extent under the influence of Poe. Maupassant and Damon Runyon have a right to their uniqueness. So has Poe.

—Buranelli, Vincent. "Fiction Themes." In *Edgar Allan Poe*. New York: Twayne Publishers, 1961 pp. 72–73.

EDWARD H. DAVIDSON ON POE'S NARRATORS

[Edward H. Davidson has been a professor of English at the University of Illinois and Harvard. His critical works include essays on Poe, Hawthorne, and colonial American writing, as well as *Hawthorne's Last Phase*, and *Jonathan Edwards: The Narrative of a Puritan Mind*. He is also the editor of two volumes of Hawthorne's manuscripts. Davidson sees Poe's narrators as caught in an endless struggle between mind and body or mind and soul, a struggle that can end only in death.]

"The Cask of Amontillado" raises, however, another question pertaining to the multiple character of the self, a question which hs been implicit throughout Poe's other studies of this theme. There is no verifiable consistency in any of these treatments of the human will and behavior; no one character is very much like any other and no single motive or action has very much relation to others. The fracture or dislocation of human faculties is different every time such an event occurs. The only permission Poe may have for such a curious psychology of human behavior is the apparent conviction he had that life consists of the disjuction of sides of the self: various elements in the human psyche or being are forever at war with each other; tragedy is always present because, in the inevitable bifurcation, one element is bound to obtain control and thereby exert such dominance that the human being is separated not only from the normal condition of a balanced selfhood but from his fellows and from the world around him. The Poe protagonist, in another respect, is compulsively driven toward death because, if life is the condition of fatal separation of the human body, mind, and spirit, death or whatever afterlife there may be is the unification of these faculties. The narrator of "The Tell-Tale Heart," who suffers and commits a crime because of the excess of emotion over intelligence, is impelled to give himself up and pay the death penalty because he may thereby return to full selfhood or primal being. Death is the completion of the life cycle; it restores that totality of being with which one began existence or which one might have had in some prior existence but which, in the inevitable chaos of this earthly life, is more and more destroyed. The tragedy (if it is a tragedy) of the Poe heroes is that they suffer from a war between their own faculties, body and mind, or mind and soul; and once that struggle has begun, it ends only with death. This disease of being is the enormous distension of any one perception or faculty at the expense of the others; and the Poe protagonists nearly all have in common the death-wish: at the end the tripartite self is able to realize its total selfhood. In death comes the full comprehension toward which Poe had moved in the poems but which he could more artfully treat, as process and intellectual activity, in the short stories.

—Davidson, Edward H. "The Tale as Allegory." In *Poe: A Critical Study*, Cambridge, MA: The Belknap Press , 1957, pp. 202–203.

JAMES W. GARGANO ON DELUSION IN THE STORY

[A professor of English at Washington and Jefferson College in Pennsylvania, James Gargano was also a Fulbright lecturer at the University of Caen. He has written extensively on nineteenth-century American writers such as Edith Wharton and Mark Twain, and is a member of the editorial board of *Poe Studies*, a journal devoted entirely to discussions of Edgar Allan Poe. "The Question of Poe's Narrators" is one of the most influential essays written on Poe, and has been widely anthologized. He describes Montresor, the narrator of "The Cask of Amontillado," as a "deluded rationalist," whose destruction of his foe Fortunato has led to his own mental and psychical disintegration.]

Evidence of Poe's "seriousness" seems to me indisputable in "The Cask of Amontillado," a tale which W. H. Auden has belittled. Far from being his author's mouthpiece, the narrator, Montresor, is one of the supreme examples in fiction of a deluded rationalist who cannot glimpse the moral implications of his planned folly. Poe's fine ironic sense makes clear that Montresor, the stalker of Fortunato, is both a compulsive and pursued man; for in committing a flawless crime against another human being, he really (like Wilson and the protagonist in "The Tell-Tale Heart") commits the worst of crimes against himself. His reasoned, cool intelligence weaves an intricate plot which, while ostensibly satisfying his revenge, despoils him of humanity. His impeccably contrived murder, his weird mask of goodness in an enterprise of evil, and his abandonment of all his life-energies in one pet project of hate convict him of a madness which he mistakes for the inspiration of genius. The brilliant masquerade setting of Poe's tale intensifies the theme of Montresor's apparently successful duplicity; Montresor's ironic appreciation of his own deviousness seems further to justify his arrogance of intellect. But the greatest irony of all, to which Montresor is never sensitive, is that the injuries supposedly perpetrated by Fortunato are illusory and that the vengeance meant for the victim recoils upon Montresor himself. In immolating Fortunato, the narrator unconsciously calls him the noble Fortunato and confesses that his own "heart grew sick." Though Montresor attributes this sickness to "the dampness of the catacombs," it is clear that his crime has begun to possess him. We see that, after fifty years, it remains the obsession of his life; the meaning of his existence resides in the tomb in which he has, symbolically, buried himself. In other words, Poe leaves little doubt that the narrator has violated his own mind and humanity, that the external act has had its destructive inner consequences.

—Gargano, James. "The Question of Poe's Narrators." *College English* 25 (1968): 180.

[Professor of American Studies at the University of Kansas, Stuart Levine has also taught at the University of Missouri and Kansas State University. He is the editor of *American Studies*, and has written multiple essays on Herman Melville, Native Americans, and Edgar Allan Poe, as well as editing an edition of Poe's short fiction. His book *The American Indian Today* was the winner of the Anisfield-Wolf Award. Here he explains the repetitions found throughout "The Cask of Amontillado" as being related to a sort of perverse religious ritual, in which Montresor plays god over his hapless victim.]

Matching the fearful economy is a fearful symmetry. The author of another of the radical readings of the tale points out that the action is framed by a pair of repetitions; at the opening, Fortunato repeats Montresor's word "Amontillado!" At the close, the situations are reversed:

> "For the love of God, Montresor!"
> "Yes," I said, "for the love of God!"

Indeed, there is a great deal of mocking repetition in the last pages of "The Cask of Amontillado." Montresor sets the tone when Fortunato asks if he is a Mason. ("A mason.") The game continues after Fortunato is chained. ("The Amontillado!" "True . . . the Amontillado.") When Fortunato screams, Montresor screams louder. When Fortunato tries to laugh the entire affair off as a prank, and says "Let us be gone," the narrator says, "Yes, . . . let us be gone." Finally comes the blasphemous mockery, "For the love of God!"

Repetition is, of course, an obvious characteristic of rituals of any type. A ritualistic language is frequently a language heavy in repetition, and a religious ritual derives a good deal of its emotional power from the repeated use of formulas. Because this tale succeeds in evoking a mythic feeling, even writers primarily concerned with analysis of technique have been moved to seek underlying meanings; certainly the ritualistic nature of these repetitive passages helps create the sense that there is something deeper than catacombs present. It will, however, be noted that the repetitions here, though they perform a somewhat similar function, are of a different sort than

those in the last sentences of *Pym*, or in the colloquies. There Poe pur-
posefully used a formulaic language to create a prophetic tone; here
Poe uses repetition for dramatic effect, but the effect is also ritualistic.

Since, in this discussion we have dealt with terms—myth and
ritual—which to some degree overlap, it would perhaps be well to
differentiate, or at least attempt to define the nature of the interrela-
tionship. In a useful discussion of the subject, Austin Warren wrote,
"For many writers, myth is the common denominator between
poetry and religion. . . . Religious myth is the large-scale authoriza-
tion of poetic metaphor." This is relevant for Poe, for he shared the
then-current notions concerning the connection between the ideal
artist and his source of inspiration; his ideal artist was a kind of god,
and practiced god-like creation. But clearly Montresor is not the
ideal artist. What he created is a murder plot. Yet that plot has the
characteristic "look" of the beautiful creations in Poe: it is complex,
it is ornate, it is *bizarre*. It will, in short, "take" all those terms which
Poe uses to characterize ideal beauty, or those terms with which
Dupin characterizes the beautiful patterns which he unravels. Mr.
Felheim, in the passage quoted above, says that Montresor "assumes
a perverted priestly function." In terms of the usual pattern of the
Poe story, such a judgment seems just, although it might be better to
use a stronger word than "priest." Poe's ideal poet-creator plays god;
Montresor, too, plays god, and were the story more overtly con-
cerned with moral issues, one might even be able to say that god-
playing is his sin.

> —Levine, Stuart. "Horror, Beauty and Involvement." In *Edgar Poe:
> Seer and Craftsman*. DeLand, FL: Everett/Edwards, 1972, pp. 85–87.

GUY DAVENPORT ON SYMBOLISM IN POE'S TALES

[Guy Davenport is a renowned essayist, whose collections
include *Da Vinci's Bicycle, A Table of Green Fields,* and *The
Geography of the Imagination.* He has also translated the
poems of Sappho and Archilochus, and wrote a study of
Ezra Pound's cantos. He is a professor of English at the
University of Kentucky. This essay was originally presented

in 1978 as a Distinguished Professor Lecture at the University of Kentucky. In it, Davenport explains how Poe's imagery is divided into three distinct spheres; the grotesque, the arabesque, and the classical, each of which has its own language of symbols. Knowing the background of these styles of description lends a deeper understanding to a reading of his tales.]

Poe titled the collection of his stories published that year *Tales of the Grotesque and Arabesque.* These two adjectives have given critics trouble for years. *Grotesque,* as Poe found it in the writings of Sir Walter Scott, means something close to *Gothic,* an adjective designating the Goths and their architecture, and what the neoclassical eighteenth century thought of medieval art in general, that it was ugly but grand. It was the fanciful decoration by the Italians of grottoes, or caves, with shells, and statues of ogres and giants from the realm of legend, that gave the word *grotesque* its meaning of *freakish, monstrous, misshapen.*

Arabesque clearly means the intricate, nonrepresentational, infinitely graceful decorative style of Islam, best known to us in their carpets, the geometric tile-work of their mosques, and their calligraphy.

Had Poe wanted to designate the components of his imagination more accurately, his title would have been, *Tales of the Grotesque, Arabesque, and Classical.* For Poe in all his writing divided all his imagery up into three distinct species.

Look back at the pictures on the wall in his ideal rooms. In one we have grottoes and a view of the Dismal Swamp: this is the grotesque mode. Then female heads in the manner of Sully: this is the classical mode. The wallpaper against which they hang is arabesque.

In the other room we had a scene of oriental luxury: the arabesque, a carnival piece spirited beyond compare (Poe means masked and costumed people, at Mardi Gras, as in "The Cask of Amontillado" and "The Masque of the Red Death"): the grotesque, and a Greek female head: the classical.

A thorough inspection of Poe's work will disclose that he performs variations and mutations of these three vocabularies of imagery. We can readily recognize those works in which a particular idiom is dominant. The great octosyllabic sonnet "To Helen," for instance, is classical, "The Fall of the House of Usher" is grotesque, and the poem "Israfel" is arabesque.

But no work is restricted to one mode; the other two are there also . . .

Were we to follow the metamorphoses of these images through all of Poe—grotesque, or Gothic; arabesque, or Islamic; classical, or Graeco-Roman—we would discover an articulate grammar of symbols, a new, as yet unread Poe. What we shall need to understand is the meaning of the symbols, and why they are constantly being translated from one imagistic idiom to another.

The clues are not difficult, or particularly arcane. Israfel for instance is an arabesque, and Roderick Usher a grotesque Orpheus; Orpheus himself does not appear in Poe in his native Greek self. But once we see Orpheus in Usher, we can then see that this masterpiece is a retelling of his myth from a point of view informed by a modern understanding of neuroses, of the inexplicable perverseness of the human will. That lute, that speaking guitar, all those books on Usher's table about journeys underground and rites held in darkness—all fit into a translation by Poe of a classical text into a Gothic one. "The Gold Bug," as Northrop Frye has seen, is strangely like the marriage of Danaë; the old black who lowers the gold bug is named Jupiter. Danaë was shut up in a treasure house and a riddle put her there.

Where do these images come from? The Mediterranean in the time of Columbus was from its western end and along its northern shore Graeco-Roman, what historians call the Latin culture, and at its eastern end, and along its southern shore, Islamic. So two thirds of Poe's triple imagery sums up the Mediterranean, and fed his imagination with its most congenial and rich portion. The Gothic style has its home in northern Europe, "my Germany of the soul" as Poe put it. He was always ambiguous about the culture with which, ironically, he is identified. Death, corruption, and dreariness inhere in the Gothic. Poe relates it to melancholia, hypersensitivity, madness, obsession, awful whirlpools in the cold sea, ancient houses spent and crumbling.

—Davenport, Guy, *The Geography of the Imagination*. New York and San Francisco: Pantheon Books, 1954, pp. 6–8.

[The author of numerous articles on Edgar Allan Poe and
other American authors, Stanley Kozikowski teaches at
Bryant College. In his study of "The Cask of Amontillado,"
Kozikowski focuses on Poe's use of irony to shed light upon
Montresor's actions, and explains the tale as driven by reli-
gious tension.]

Poe evokes approximately the same historical time in another of his
popular tales, "The Pit and the Pendulum," where it is evident that
he does not emerge as a Catholic partisan. Similarly, Montresor is
unfavorably presented as the perpetrator of a secret vengeance taken
against a member of a group unsympathetic to the dispossessed
Catholic royalty. And while under the protection of Napoleon,
whose brother headed the Grand Orient Lodge of Paris, one such as
Fortunato might well have gained, and insultingly so, what one such
as Montresor had lost: admiration, respect, wealth, eminence, and
the affection of others. Poe also has Montresor characterize his
adversary as a Machiavellian—as one who is "respected and even
feared" (a wisely political status in *Il Principe*) and especially in
being of a group whose "enthusiasm is adopted to suit the time and
opportunity" (a prescriptive behavior for gaining power and wealth
in *Il Principe*). Montresor's latter observation is one of several
ironies which emerge from that gap between the actions and words
of the narrator. The Catholic avenger, punishing an enthusiastic
opportunist, becomes in his calculation of vengeance a chance-
seeking zealot himself. And this opportunism, like Fortunato's, takes
Montresor to a dead fault. His vengeance, after all, has served only to
satisfy a retribution carefully prepared in advance, and, in doing so,
it pretty much loses sight of what had prompted it in the first place.
The single result is Montresor's narration itself, long in coming,
which fails to examine the perfect futility which is both its cause and
subject. All that Montresor has gained from his deed, in the ironic
scheme of Poe's art, is the opportunity to recite his story in a manner
leaving him oblivious to its dreadful implication. As the symbology
of his family arms denotes, one meaning of triumph and another of
defeat emerge: the heralded iconology of Christ's sacrificial victory
over orginal sin and its profaned equivalent, the unconscious irony
of Montresor's redress of a wrong at his own expense. We may

observe in the latter respect that Poe evokes the emblematic snake in Fortunator's recoiling at the sight of the trowel. Similar effects of irony in the tale illustrate, vividly, how one redemptive prospect after another has become diminished for Montresor. Hence, "impunity" and retribution are not viewed as the Catholic Montresor should see them, but as the temporal limit within which he might escape or gain punishment. The "flambeaux" do not cast truth's light; their dim glow illuminates only the passing show of evil action. The jingling of the bells on Fortunato's cap seems to conclude ceremonially, as if in ironic answer to Montresor's perverse Masonic ritual, with a counter parody, perhaps now of the Santus bells, rung to bring on the most holy quiet during the Catholic Mass, but now leaving Montresor with the sickening silence of his sin. And the conclusion of the Requiem Mass, which Montresor intones—"*In pace requiescat*"—serves to remind the reader that Montresor, by his summons of the dead past, has disturbed *once more* the bones of the departed, and by denying himself the chance to confess, he has denied himself perhaps the last prospect of his own soul's repose.

—Kozikowski, Stanley J. "A Reconsideration of Poe's 'The Cask of Amontillado.'" In *The American Transcendental Quarterly: A Journal of New England Writers.* Kingston, University of Rhode Island, 1978: pp 276–277.

Plot Summary of
"The Pit and the Pendulum"

"The Pit and the Pendulum," on the surface the tale of a man tormented by outside forces and the devilish imagination of other men, is also a nightmare, an evocation of the power of the imagination to conquer the rational mind. In it the narrator progresses through deepening levels of unconsciousness, from swoon to dream to delirium to madness, and finally into unconsciousness. The story takes the form of a spiral leading inexorably inward to the terrifying and indescribable pit. It is here that Poe's psychological insight is most evident. For the pit is both the physical chasm in the floor of the narrator's prison and the dark abyss of the unknown that lurks within the mind. The narrator claims, hopes, desperately believes that humans possess immortality because there is some level of consciousness even beyond the grave. Yet this tale, with its alternating levels of sanity and madness, of control and powerlessness, questions the ability of the mind to resist the dark unknown of the imagination.

The story opens upon the trial of the narrator, who has been brought before the Spanish Inquisition for an unknown crime. As the judges pronounce the sentence of death, the narrator's consciousness wavers in and out, fading finally into a swoon as "all sensations appeared swallowed up in a mad rushing descent of the soul into Hades." At this point in the narrative he insists that all of his consciousness was *not* lost, that even in the deepest insensibility the mind retains some of its powers. This is a key moment in the tale, when the narrator discusses how the unconscious mind provides a glimpse into the "gulf beyond," the unplumbed world of the unknown. Poe, the poet of the subliminal, wrestles here with the difficulty of describing what imagination is, of explaining how it intersects with the rational, daylight senses of the conscious mind.

The narrator awakens to find himself in total darkness, and is overwhelmed with the fear that he might have been buried alive in a tomb. He investigates his surroundings and finds that he is in a cold, slimy vault made of irregular panels. He determines to find out how big the chamber is, and begins to crawl around its perimeter. Crossing the floor, the stumbles and falls just at the edge of a gaping pit. Had he walked just a step more, he would have fallen to his death.

Overcome by fatigue, he sleeps, and on arising drinks and eats, only to discover that the water was drugged. He falls unconscious, and awakens to find himself strapped to a wooden platform in the middle of the chamber. A "sulphurous lustre" reveals walls painted with "the hideous and repulsive devices to which the charnel superstition of the monks has given rise." Throughout the tale, Poe maintains a decidedly anti-clerical tone, emphasizing his view that the Church has a negative effect upon human imagination.

The narrator looks upwards to see a painted figure of Time holding a huge pendulum, like a razor-sharp scythe. He also sees enormous rats running about the chamber, attracted by the bits of meat left on his plate. When he looks back at the ceiling, he is appalled to see that the glittering blade has descended, and is designed to "cross the region of the heart." He will die ever so slowly, with the pendulum of Time cutting his chest open to the heart. He struggles vainly to free himself, choking on the "long, long hours of horror more than mortal." He smells the sharp scent of the steel in his nostrils and falls into bouts of madness, only to be rescued by the sudden stirrings of hope.

"For the first time during many hours—or perhaps days—I *thought*." The powers of reason have leapt forth against the nightmare with all the "keen, collected calmness of despair." Taking up the fragments of meat, the narrator rubs them over the bandages tied tightly across his body. The rats swarm forward, gnawing frantically at the smeared cloth. Just as the descending blade slices into his flesh, the straps part under the sharp teeth of the rats and the narrator slithers free.

Yet his tormentors have watched every movement, and his freedom is illusory. The pendulum is withdrawn into the ceiling, and a horrible radiance begins to fill the chamber. "For many minutes of dreamy and trembling abstraction, I busied myself in vain, unconnected conjecture." Again the narrator's powers of rational though have been thwarted, and again he begins to descend into unconsciousness. The paintings on the walls begin to glow with an intense brilliance, as devilish eyes glare from every direction. A "suffocating odor" pervades the vault, and the walls begin to move irresistibly inwards. The narrator is pushed ever closer to the pit, whose occult horrors have been revealed by the fiery glare. "For a wild moment, did my spirit refuse to comprehend the meaning of what I saw. At length it forced—it wrestled its way into my soul—it burned itself upon my shuddering reason. . . . oh! any horror but this!" Yet we do not know what is revealed in the pit, what dreadful vision overwhelms the narrator. It is part of Poe's genius that in a tale of the terrors of the imagination, he leaves the form of the ultimate dread for our own imaginations to conjure up.

The walls press ever closer and closer to the pit, with the narrator wailing in desperation on the edge. Then, at the last moment, just as he gives way to despair and topples into the pit, there is a blast of trumpets and he is saved by the invading French army. While this ending may seem artificial and absurd to us, to the Romantics such a strange, bizarre denouement would be enormously effective. Reality is strange, and the tale that captures this sense of the unexpected would be valued for its rhetorical power.

Throughout this tale, the narrator is tormented as much by his imagination as by the actual tortures of the Inquisition. Whatever he envisions; total darkness, a gap in the bandages just in the path of the descending blade, a death worse than that of the pendulum, he encounters. His tortures are foreshadowed by his own fantasy. This sense of claustrophobia, of a mind trapped within itself, is accentuated by his physical isolation in the vault. Other people exist only as sounds and passing visions of terror. They are the agents of his doom, but it is a doom he has metaphorically created within his mind. His final fall into the pit is as much a fall into madness, the destruction of identity and consciousness, as it is into an actual chasm. Poe has achieved his crucial unity of effect, of unrelieved torture and suspense, dragging the narrator and reader ever deeper into the dreadful chambers of the Inquisition. But the true terror is that of the horrors of an imagination falling out of control. ❀

List of Characters in
"The Pit and the Pendulum"

Narrator

Sentenced to death for an unknown crime by the Spanish Inquisition, the narrator remains a nameless enigma to the reader. He is clearly intelligent, as shown by his escape from the deadly pendulum, but his consciousness and intellect are shattered repeatedly by his nightmarish situation. In many ways the narrator seems to create his own torments, just as a dreamer caught in a nightmare does. He imagines the worst that could have befallen him, utter darkness, only to find upon opening his eyes that this is the case. He imagines that the straps crossing his chest will *not* be cut by the descending blade, only to find that they are not. It is as though the narrator, and the reader with him, are caught in a trap of the mind, a torture of the imagination from which they can only be freed by an outside force. The mind is not enough to escape the nightmare of the mind alone, and it is only by the greatest (and most suspiciously fortuitous) good luck that the narrator escapes at all.

Other Characters

Although other characters (the judges of the Spanish Inquisition, the guards in the dungeon, the rescuing army of LaSalle) make brief appearances, they act only as shadows in "The Pit and the Pendulum." Because Poe's emphasis here is on the isolation of the central character, it is essential that he be cut off from contact with any other humans. He communicates only with the hideous rats of his dark chamber, a situation causing simultaneous disgust and pity in the reader. Interestingly, it is when the narrator is at his most conscious and active, when he escapes from the pendulum, that he becomes most like the rats, slipping stealthily out from under the glittering blade. ✾

Critical Views on
"The Pit and the Pendulum"

N. BRYLLION FAGIN ON POE'S CREATION OF A "SINGLE
UNIFIED EFFECT"

[A president of the Edgar Allan Poe society of Baltimore, N.
Bryllion Fagin (1862–1972) taught English Literature at the
University of Baltimore and Johns Hopkins University, and
was the director of the Johns Hopkins Playhouse. In addition to *The Histrionic Mr. Poe,* which was a landmark in Poe
criticism, Fagin also co-edited, with John Esten Cooke, *Poe
as a Literary Critic.* He is also the author of books on Sher-
wood Anderson and William Bartram. Fagin addresses Poe's
interest in creating a "maximum of effect with a minimum
of means" by tracing the influences of poetry and drama in
Poe's work.]

For Poe then, the central problem was—as C. Alphonso Smith for-
mulated it forty years ago—"How may I produce the maximum of
effect with the minimum of means?" What means he ultimately
resorted to, and with what success, can be ascertained only by a
careful reading and examination of the stories themselves. Here it is
pertinent to call attention to the resemblance of the problem to the
one which confronts every practitioner of an art, or rather a group
of arts, generally considered different from that of fiction writing:
the art or arts of the theatre. It is the production of effect in which
every actor, director, stage designer, electrician, and costumer is
engaged. And economy of means by which to produce this effect is a
basic principle in the theatre. Everything on a stage, every word,
movement, and gesture of the actor, every piece of decoration, furni-
ture, or prop, must contribute to the creation of the preconceived
effects in the minds of the actor and designer, and all these effects
must blend into the final totality which the director is envisaged.
Therefore every object, movement, word, and tone uttered—like
every word and sentence in a story—must be purposeful and "tend
to the outbringing" of the desired effect.

If the analogy does not at first glance seem to include Poe's principle of brevity, it nevertheless holds. For brevity, involving both a

certain minimum and maximum duration, is imbedded in totality of effect. Every theatre man knows that the slightest digression or unnecessary prolongation of a scene or moment on the stage is weakening if not ruinous to a performance. And surely a play in the theatre fulfills Poe's requirement that a story must be read at one sitting. Theatre audiences know better than any reader, sitting in the privacy of his room, "the immense force derivable from totality."

Poe's ideas on the short story were undoubtedly derived, to a considerable extent at least, from his contemplation of the processes underlying the creation of poetry, and especially lyric poetry. Yet his knowledge of dramatic practices and his native theatrical flair affected all of his theories and practices. The means he employed for bringing about the effects he preconceived for his stories were largely theatrical. His plots, whatever their nature or merits, were constructed with an eye to effectiveness as dramatic or melodramatic fables; his locales were for the most part so many stage settings; his characters were, in his own frequently employed designation, "dramatis personae"; his dialogue—weak as realistic transcription of idiomatic speech—was emotionally intense and in its own peculiar way, if not actually stage worthy, at least "stagy"; and his devices for blending visual and auditory elements into exciting climaxes were deliberately theatrical. Whatever values one may find in Poe's stores—psychological, symbolical, autobiographical—one can hardly appreciate the effectiveness of his narratives without an awareness of their indebtedness to the arts of the theatre.

—Fagin, N. Bryllion. "A Skilful Literary Artist." In *The Histrionic Mr. Poe*. Baltimore: The Johns Hopkins Press, 1949, pp. 164–166.

WILLIAM CARLOS WILLIAMS ON POE'S AMERICAN NATURE

[The founder of the Objectivist school of American poetry, William Carlos Williams (1883–1963) was also a practicing pediatrician in Rutherford, New Jersey. His volume of poems, *Pictures from Breughel*, won a Pulitzer Prize in 1964. In this essay, Williams explains the peculiarly American nature of Poe's work, the "re-awakened genius of place" and bursting strength of a new literature.]

Poe's work strikes by its scrupulous originality, *not* "originality" in the bastard sense, but in its legitimate sense of solidity which goes back to the ground, a conviction that he *can* judge within himself. These things the French were *ready* to perceive and quick to use to their advantage: a new point from which to readjust the trigono-metric measurements of literary form.

It is the New World, or to leave that for the better term, it is a *new locality* that is in Poe assertive; it is America, the first great burst through to expression of a re-awakened genius of *place*.

Poe gives the sense for the first time in America, that literature is *serious,* not a matter of courtesy but of truth.

The aspect of his critical statements as a whole, from their hun-dred American titles to the inmost structure of his sentences, is that of a single gesture, not avoiding the trivial, to sweep all worthless chaff aside. It is a movement, first and last to clear the GROUND.

There is a flavor of provincialism that is provincialism in the plainness of his reasoning upon elementary grammatical, syntac-tical, and prosodic grounds which awakened Lowell's derision. But insistence upon primary distinctions, that seems coldly academic, was in this case no more than evidence of a strong impluse to begin at the beginning. Poe was unsophisticated, when contrasted with the puerile sophistications of a Lowell. It is a *beginning* he has in mind, a juvenescent *local* literature. By this he avoids the clownish turn of trying to join, contrary to every reasonable impulsion, a literature (the English) with which he had no actual connection and which might be presumed, long since, to have passed that beginning which to the new condition was requisite.

The local causes shaping Poe's genius were two in character: the necessity for a fresh beginning, backed by a native vigor of extraordi-nary proportions—with the corollary, that all "colonial imitation" must be swept aside. This was the conscious force which rose in Poe as innumerable timeless insights resulting, by his genius, in firm statements on the character of form, profusely illustrated by his practices; and, *second* the immediate effect of the locality upon the first, upon his nascent impulses, upon his original thrusts; tormenting the depths into a surface of bizarre designs by which he's known and which are *not at all* the major point in question.

Yet BOTH influences were determined by the locality, which, in the usual fashion, finds its mind swayed by the results of its stupidity rather than by a self-interest bred of greater wisdom. As with all else in America, the value of Poe's genius to OURSELVES must be *uncovered* from our droppings, or at least uncovered from the "protection" which it must have raised about itself to have survived in any form among us—where everything is quickly trampled.

—Williams, William Carlos. "Edgar Allan Poe." In *In the American Grain*. New York: Albert & Charles Boni, 1925, pp. 216–219.

CHARLES E. MAY ON DREAMS AND REALITY IN THE STORY

[Editor of over 100 essays on short fiction, Charles May is the consulting editor for *Short Story*. He is also the editor of *Short Story Theories* and *Twentieth-Century European Short Story: An Annotated Bibliography*. He teaches English at California State University at Long Beach. In this study of "The Pit and the Pendulum," May outlines the complex interplay of dreaming and waking, consciousness and unconsciousness, in the narrator.]

The story is a Poe paradigm. Focusing on a character under sentence of death and aware of it, it moves the character into a concrete dilemma that seems to "stand for" a metaphysical situation in an ambiguous way that suggests its "dreamy," "indeterminate" nature. In this story we find the most explicit statement in Poe's fiction of his sense of the blurry line between dream and reality. The narrator considers that although when we awake even from the soundest sleep, "we break the gossamer web of some dream," the web is so flimsy that a second later we forget we have dreamed at all. But sometimes, perhaps much later, memories of the details of the dream come back and we do not know where they have come from. This sense of having a memory of that which did not in fact occur is central to the story's ambiguity, for as the narrator tries to remember his experience, it is not clear whether the memory is of a real event or a dream event that has been forgotten.

He does not know in what state he is; the only thing he does know is that he is not dead, for he says, "Such a supposition, notwithstanding what we read in fiction, is altogether inconsistent with real existence—but where and in what state was I?" The narrator's task is simply to save himself, but in order to survive he must know where he is; the first crucial task he undertakes is to try to orient himself. However, his efforts are complicated by his moving back and forth between sleep and waking; each time he falls asleep, he must reorient himself all over again. This explains why even after trying to demarcate his position, he awakes and, instead of going on forward, retraces his steps and thus overestimates the size of his cell.

Like the protagonist in "A Descent into the Maelström," he is preoccupied with curiosity about the mere physical nature of his surroundings, taking a "wild interest in trifles." Nonetheless, in spite of his deliberative efforts, it is the accident of tripping that saves him from the pit the first time. Waking from another interlude of sleep, he finds himself bound and notes above him a picture of time, synonymous with death, carrying not the image of a scythe, but rather an actual pendulum that sweeps back and forth. In this situation, surrounded by the repulsive rats, with the scythe of time and thus death over his head, he again moves back and forth between the states of sensibility and insensibility. This pattern of moving in and out of consciousness is much like the pattern in "Ligeia" and is typical of Poe, for in such an alternating state consciousness has some of the characteristics of unconsciousness and vice versa; one state is imbued with the qualities of the other state. As a result, Poe's stories are neither solely like the consciousness of realism, nor the projective unconsciousness of romance. Later, when the narrator totters on the brink of the pit, the walls rush back and an outstretched arm catches him as he falls. The ending is not an ending at all, but rather the beginning of waking life, the movement from the gossamer dream or nightmare that constitutes the story itself.

—May, Charles E. "Alternate Realms of Reality." In *Edgar Allan Poe: A Study of Short Fiction*. Boston: Twayne Publishers, 1991, pp.96–97

GERALD KENNEDY ON PREMATURE BURIAL AND THE STORY

[Winner of the 1978 Pushcart Prize for his essay "Roland Barthes, Autobiography and the End of Writing," J. Gerald Kennedy is the author of *Poe, Death and the Life of Writing, Imagining Paris: Exile, Writing and American Identity,* and *The Astonished Traveler: William Darby, Frontier Geographer and Man of Letters.* He has taught at Louisiana State University at Baton Rouge, and was a Fulbright lecturer at the University of Lille. He examines the narrator of "The Pit and the Pendulum," who is like Madeleine Usher in being simultaneously "dead and alive," and explains the tale as one in a long series from Poe of premature burials.]

Poe perceived premature burial as an equivalent to death itself not simply because of its inherent lethality, but also because he believed all burials to be "living" insofar as consciousness extended beyond physical death. In "The Pit and the Pendulum" he declared, "Even in the grave all *is not* lost. Else there is no immortality for man. Arousing from the most profound of slumbers, we break the gossamer web of *some* dream." Much of the power of this celebrated tale derives from the uncertain relationship between consciousness and death. With his opening words—"I was sick—sick unto death with that long agony"—the narrator evokes the psychic environment of death anxiety and upon receiving the death sentence loses consciousness—only to recover it in a manner characteristic of the premature-burial narrative:

> Very suddenly there came back to my soul motion and sound—the tumultuous motion of the heart, and, in my ears, the sound of its beating. Then a pause in which all is blank. Then again sound, and motion, and touch—a tingling sensation pervading my frame. Then the mere consciousness of existence, without thought—a condition which lasted long. Then, very suddenly, *thought,* and shuddering terror, and earnest endeavor to comprehend my true state.

Not for a moment does he suppose himself actually dead, yet through his own anticipations of death he intuits the desperation of his situation, and a fearful idea enters his mind: that he will find himself "impeded by the walls of a tomb." The fear that he has been entombed alive brings to mind all of the associations by which death is imaged. Though he subsequently determines his receptacle to be a dungeon, the narrator continues to experience his confinement as a premature burial. He is simultaneously a dead man (condemned to death) and a living victim, and his elemental struggle seems to unfold at the threshold of consciousness itself, for survival depends upon coherence of thought in the face of horrors dredged up from the unconscious. Like the victim of premature interment, he feels the hopelessness of his predicament; he is oppressed by "the intensity of the darkness"; amid the gloom he descries the imagery of the burial vault, "hideous and repulsive devices" of a "charnel superstition . . . the figures of fiends in aspects of menace, with skeleton forms." The convergence of the walls evokes once again the panic of fatal enclosure, and only the arrival of a deus ex machina (a resurrection man, as it were) saves him from death-in-life. Indeed, for all its historical trappings as a tale of the Inquisition, "The Pit and the Pendulum" amounts to an elaborate fantasy of burial alive, drawing its claustrophobic intensity from the sense of impending annihilation.

—Kennedy, J. Gerald "Notes from Underground: Premature Burial." In *Poe Death, and the Life of Writing*. New Haven and London: Yale University Press, 1978, pp. 53–54

Charles Baudelaire on Intellect and Imagination in Poe

[A French poet and critic, Charles Baudelaire (1821–1867) foreshadowed Symbolist poetry, which strove to look anew at the world, finding beauty in lowly areas of life and corruption in what was generally considered beautiful. His collection of poems, *Les Fleurs du Mal* (1857), was accused of obscenity and he was accused of moral deviance. His critical works include *Curiosités esthétiques* and *L'art Romantique*. Baudelaire was one of the first French writers to recognize Poe's genius, and was his first translator into French. In this selection, he discussed how Poe combined intellect and imagination in his work to achieve an essential unity of effect.]

In a country where the idea of utility, the most hostile in the world to the idea of beauty, dominates and takes precedence over everything, the perfect critic will be the most *respectable,* that is to say the one whose tendencies and desires will best approximate the tendencies and desires of his public—the one who, confusing the intellectual faculties of the writer and the categories of writing, will assign to all a single goal—the one who will seek in a book of poetry the means of perfecting conscience. Naturally he will become all the less concerned with the real, the positive beauties of poetry; he will be all the less shocked by imperfections and even by faults in execution. Edgar Poe, on the contrary, dividing the world of the mind into *pure Intellect, Taste,* and *moral Sense,* applied criticism in accordance with the category to which the object of his analysis belonged. He was above all sensitive to perfection of plan and to correctness of execution; taking apart literary works like defective pieces of machinery (considering the goal that they wished to attain), noting carefully the flaws of workmanship; and when he passed to the detail of the work, to its plastic expression, in a word, to style, examining meticulously and without omissions the faults of prosody, the grammatical errors and all the mass of dross which, among writers who are not artists, besmirch the best intentions and deform the most noble conceptions.

For him, Imagination is the queen of faculties; but by his word he understands something greater than that which is understood by the average reader. Imagination is not fantasy; nor is it sensibility, although it may be difficult to conceive of an imaginative man who would be lacking in sensibility. Imagination is an almost divine faculty which perceives immediately and without philosophical methods the inner and secret relations of things, the correspondences and the analogies. The honors and functions which he grants to this faculty give it such value (at least when the thought of the author has been well understood) that a scholar without imagination appears only as a pseudo-scholar, or at least as an incomplete scholar.

Among the literary domains where imagination can obtain the most curious results, can harvest treasures, not the richest, the most precious (those belong to poetry), but the most numerous and the most varied, there is one of which Poe is especially fond; it is the short story. It has the immense advantage over the novel of vast proportions that its brevity adds to the intensity of effect. This type of reading, which can be accomplished in one sitting, leaves in the mind a more powerful impression than a broken reading, often interrupted by the worries of business and the cares of social life. The unity of impression, the totality of effect is an immense advantage which can give to this type of composition a very special superiority, to such an extent that an extremely short story (which is doubtless a fault) is even better than an extremely long story. The artist, if he is skillful, will not adapt his thoughts to the incidents, but, having conceived deliberately and at leisure an effect to be produced, will invent the incidents, will combine the events most suitable to bring about the desired effect. If the first sentence is not written with the idea of preparing this final impression, the work has failed from the start. There must not creep into the entire composition a single word which is not intentional, which does not tend, directly or indirectly, to complete the premeditated design.

—Baudelaire, Charles Pierre. "New Notes on Edgar Poe: 1857." In *Baudelaire on Poe.* State College, PA: Bald Eagle Press, 1952. pp. 133–135.

Works by
Edgar Allan Poe

Books

Tamerlane and Other Poems. 1827.

El Aaraaf, Tamerlane and Minor Poems. 1829.

Poems, Second Edition. 1831.

The Narrative of Arthur Gordon Pym. 1838.

The Conchologist's First Book. 1839.

Tales of the Grotesque and Arabesque. 2 vols. 1840.

The Prose Romances of Edgar A. Poe. 1843.

The Raven and Other Poems. 1845.

Tales. 1845.

Eureka: A Prose Poem. 1848.

The Works of the Late Edgar Allan Poe, with a Memoir by Rufus Wilmot Griswold and Notices of his Life and Genius by Nathaniel Parker Willis and James Russell Lowell. 4 vols. 1850–1856.

Works about
Edgar Allan Poe

Beebe, Maurice. *Ivory Towers and Sacred Founts: The Artist as Hero in Fiction from Goethe to Joyce.* New York: New York University Press, 1964.

Benton, Richard P. "Poe's 'The Cask of Amontillado.'" *Studies in Short Fiction* 28:2 (1991): 183–194.

Bloom, Harold, ed. *The Tales of Poe.* New York: Chelsea House Publishers, 1987.

Bonaparte, Marie. *The Life and Works of Edgar Allan Poe.* Translated by John Rodker. London: Imago, 1949

Broussard, Louis. *The Measure of Poe.* Norman: University of Oklahoma Press, 1969.

Buranelli, Vincent. *Edgar Allan Poe.* Boston: Twayne, 1977.

Cavell, Stanley. *In Quest of the Ordinary: Lines of Skepticism and Romanticism.* Chicago: University of Chicago Press, 1988.

Carlson, Eric, ed. W. *The Recognition of Edgar Allan Poe: Selected Criticism Since 1829.* Ann Arbor: The University of Michigan Press, 1966.

Brooks, Cleanth. "Edgar Allan Poe as Interior Decorator." *Ventures* 8:2 (1960): 41–46.

Davidson, Edward H. *Poe: A Critical Study.* Cambridge, Massachusetts: The Belknap Press of Harvard University Press, 1966.

Dayan, Joan. *Fables of Mind: An Inquiry into Poe's Fiction.* New York: Oxford University Press, 1987.

Dedmond, Francis P. "'The Cask of Amontillado' and the War of the Literati." *Modern Language Quarterly* 15 (1954): 137–146.

Derrida, Jacques. "The Purveyor of Truth." *Yale French Studies* 52 (1976): 31–113.

Eliot, T. S. *From Poe to Valéry.* New York: Harcourt, Brace and World, 1948.

Fagin, N. Bryllion. *The Histrionic Mr. Poe.* Baltimore: The Johns Hopkins Press, 1949.

Fisher, Benjamin Franklin IV, ed. *Poe at Work: Seven Textual Studies.* Baltimore: Edgar Allan Poe Society, 1978.

Frieden, Ken. *Genius and Monologue.* Ithaca, New York: Cornell University Press, 1985.

Gargano, James. "The Question of Poe's Narrator's." *College English* 25 (1963): 177–181.

Halliburton, David. *Edgar Allan Poe: A Phenomenological View.* Princeton: Princeton University Press, 1973.

Hammond, John R. *An Edgar Allan Poe Companion: A Guide to the Short Stories, Romances and Essays.* London: Macmillan, 1981.

Harris, Kathryn Montgomery. "Ironic Revenge in Poe's 'The Cask of Amontillado.'" *Studies in Short Fiction* 6 (1969): 333–335.

Hirsch, David. H. "The Pit and the Apocalypse." *Sewanee Review* 76 (1968): 632–652.

Hoffman, Daniel. *Poe Poe Poe Poe Poe Poe Poe.* New York: Doubleday, 1973.

Howarth, William L. ed. *Twentieth Century Interpretations of Poe's Tales: A Collection of Critical Essays.* Englewood Cliffs, New Jersey: Prentice-Hall, Inc., 1971.

Hyslop, Lois and Francis E. Hyslop Jr., eds. *Baudelaire on Poe.* State College, Pennsylvania: Bald Eagle Press, 1952.

Kozikowsky, Stanely J. "A Reconsideration of Poe's 'The Cask of Amontillado.'" *American Transcendental Quarterly* 39 (1978): 269–280.

Kennedy, J. Gerald. *Poe, Death and the Life of Writing.* New Haven: Yale University Press, 1987.

Ketterer, David. *The Rationale of Deception in Poe.* Baton Rouge: Louisiana State University Press, 1979.

Krutch, Joseph W. *Edgar Allan Poe: A Study in Genius.* New York: Russell and Russell, 1926.

Levin, Harry. *The Power of Blackness: Hawthorne, Poe, Melville.* New York: Alfred A. Knopf, 1958.

Levine, Stuart. *Edgar Poe: Seer and Craftsman.* DeLand, Florida: Everett/Edwards, Inc., 1972.

Levy, Maurice. "Poe and the Gothic Tradition." *ESQ* 18:1 (1972): 19–25.

Muller, John P., and William J. Richardson, eds. *The Purloined Poe: Lacan, Derrida and Psychoanalytic Reading.* Baltimore: Johns Hopkins Univerisity Press, 1988.

Pollin, Burton R. *Discoveries in Poe.* Notre Dame: University of Notre Dame Press, 1970.

Pope-Hennessey, Una. *Edgar Allan Poe, 1809–1849.* London: Macmillan, 1934.

Quinn, Arthur Hobson. *Edgar Allan Poe: A Critical Biography.* New York: Appleton-Century-Crofts, 1942.

Quinn, Patrick F. *The French Face of Edgar Poe.* Carbondale: Southern Illinois University Press, 1957.

Regan, Robert, ed. *Poe: A Collection of Critical Essays.* Englewood Cliffs, New Jersey: Prentice-Hall, Inc., 1967.

Rosenheim, Shawn, and Stephen Rachman, eds. *The American Face of Edgar Allan Poe.* Baltimore: Johns Hopkins University Press, 1995.

Saliba, David. *The Psychology of Fear: The Nightmare Formula of Edgar Allan Poe.* Lanham, Maryland: University Press of America, 1980.

Shulman, Robert. "Poe and the Powers of the Mind." *ELH* 37:2 (1970): 245–262.

Silverman, Kenneth, ed. *New Essays on Poe's Major Tales.* Cambridge: Cambridge University Press, 1993.

Silverman, Kenneth. *Edgar A. Poe: Mournful and Never-Ending Remembrance.* New York: HarperCollins, 1991.

Smith, A.G. "The Psychological Context of Three Tales by Poe." *Journal of American Studies* 7:3 (1973): 279–288.

St. Armand, Barton. "Usher Unveiled: Poe and Gnosticism." *Poe Studies* 5:1 (1972): 8–9.

Stein, William Bysshe. "The Twin Motif in 'The Fall of the House of Usher.'" *Modern Language Notes* 75 (1960): 109–111.

Stovall, Floyd. *Edgar Poe the Poet: Essays New and Old on the Man and His Work.* Charlottesville: University Press of Virginia, 1969.

Thompson, Gary R. *Poe's Fiction: Romantic Irony in the Gothic Tales.* Madison: University of Wisconsin Press, 1973.

Voloshin, Beverly. "Transcendence Downwards: Usher and Ligeia." *Modern Language Studies* 18:3 (1988): 18–29.

Walker, I.M. ed. *Edgar Allan Poe: The Critical Heritage.* London: Routledge and K. Paul, 1986.

Woodson, Thomas, ed. *Twentieth-Century Interpretations of "The Fall of the House of Usher."* Englewood Cliffs, New Jersey: Prentice-Hall, 1969.

Index of
Themes and Ideas

POE, EDGAR ALLAN: American nature of, 74–76; beauty in prose and poems of, 37–38; biography of, 12–14; characters of, 21–23, 59–60; Conan Doyle and, 23–24; Rider Haggard and, 24; histrionic element and, 73–74; influence of, 23–24; intellect and imagination of, 79–81; literary inadequacy of, 9–11; mythic inventiveness of, 9–11; narrators of, 60–61; nightmare and, 10–11; premature burial and, 78–79; symbolism and, 64–66; time and, 46–47; H. G. Wells and, 24

"TELL-TALE HEART, THE," 9, 14, 40–53, 58; critical views on, 46–53; Evil Eye in, 47, 48–49, 50; multiple character of the self in, 61; narrator in, 40, 42–43, 44, 45, 46, 47, 49–51, 52–53, 61, 62; nightmare and, 10, 40–41; Oedipal struggle in, 47–49; old man in, 40–41, 42, 44, 46, 47–49, 50, 51, 52–53; plot summary of, 40–43; police in, 40, 41, 42, 45; realism and sanity in, 52–53; secrecy and knowledge in, 49–51; time in, 46, 47–49

"TO HELEN," 65–66

"WILLIAM WILSON," 37, 47, 58, 59, 62